MAIN

MOSES

MOSES

A NARRATIVE

ANTHONY BURGESS

F
252768

STONEHILL PUBLISHING CO.

NEW YORK

First published in the United States by the Stonehill Publishing Company, a division of Stonehill Communications, Inc., 38 East 57 Street, New York, N.Y. 10022.

First published in Great Britain by Dempsey & Squires (Publishers) Ltd., 8 Berwick Street, London W1.

ISBN: 0-88373-043-X (USA)
ISBN: 0-86044-000-1 (UK)
Library of Congress Catalog Card Number: 76-13266

Book Design by Kenneth Miyamoto.

First Printing
Printed in the USA

FOREWORD

A FEW years ago I was commissioned, along with Vittorio Bonicelli and Gianfranco de Bosio, to provide the script for a television series on the birth, life and death of the prophet Moses. I found collaboration difficult and was forced to work entirely on my own, leaving emendation, addition and subtraction to be more or less improvised—by Bonicelli, de Bosio, who was the director, Vincenzo Labella, the producer, the actors Burt Lancaster and Anthony Quayle—while filming proceeded in Israel. The major aesthetic problem was a linguistic one, as it always is with historical or mythical subjects, and I found the only way out of the problem was to precede the assembly of a shooting script with a more or less literary production—this sort of epic poem you have now in your hands. To have written *Moses* first as a prose novel would have entailed the setting up of a somewhat cumbersome mechanism, in which the devices of "naturalism" would have led me to an unwholesome prosaism both in dialogue and *récit*. Verse moves more quickly, and the rhythm of verse permits of a mode of speech midway between the mythical and the colloquial. Out of this homely epic I made my script, but the poem, such as it is, remains and is here for your reading.

If some of the devices used seem close to the cinematic, that is because I had a film in mind while working on a piece of literature. On the other hand, narrative verse—as you can see from *Aurora Leigh* as well as the *Odyssey*—anticipates the cinema. Perhaps the most ambitious film script ever written is Thomas Hardy's *The Dynasts*, which was completed before even the first crude film had been shown. John Collier recently showed how filmable *Paradise Lost* is, though his script was, sadly, specifically intended for "the cinema of the mind." Novels are heavily set in their chosen time and place and resist cinematic adaptation more than filmmakers will permit themselves to realize. Epics have more to do with wings than with walking, just like films.

None of us will ever see a film of *Beowulf* or of *The Ring and the Book*. We will have to put up instead with impossible adaptations of Tolstoy, Proust, even Joyce—all of which will be artistic as well as financial failures. But here at least you have an epic that became a film, and a not unsuccessful one. Of course, I was lucky to have the Bible behind me.

Rome, Epiphany
1976

1 | THE BONDAGE

So Joseph came to die, in some pain, dreaming he was lying
On a thorny bed called Canaan (drought and famine
And they went into Egypt and in Egypt they prospered),
Being a hundred and ten years old, and they embalmed him,
And he was put in a coffin in Egypt, being a
Prince of Egypt, the Israelite Joseph a prince of
Egypt. So Joseph died, the pain passing,
Smiling on the fulfillment: Egypt the promised land,
Brown tough shepherds and plump laughing wives
And sons like swords and daughters like date trees,
Children tumbling like lambs, the benison of mud.
Not all shepherds and shepherds' wives—
Some rose high, though not so high as Joseph,
Becoming priests of the gods, Egypt having many gods,
Officers with seals of their office, officers
On horseback leading troops, gentlemen,
Ladies, but mostly men and women in the
Good air of the delta, lambs and children frisking.
And the children of Israel were fruitful and increased abundantly,
And multiplied, and waxed exceeding mighty,
And the land was filled with them, filled with the
Tribe of Jacob and of Reuben, Simeon, Levi,
Judah, Iassachar, Zebulun, Benjamin,
Dan, Naphtali, Gad, Asher,
The tribes keeping their distance one from another,
But all with a memory of a dead land called Canaan
And of a dead prince or god of Egypt called Joseph.

Now there arose up a new king over Egypt,
Which knew not Joseph. And he said unto his people:
Behold, the people of the children of Israel
Are more and mightier than we.
The great intellectual eroded face of the Pharaoh,
The tired eroded voice, the wasted body in gold cloth,
The ringed claws grasping the sphinx arms
Of the pharaonic throne, aromatic gums asmoke,
Slaves with feather fans, effigies, effigies,
All empty-eyed. The councilors listened.
"Their men are bursting with seed. Their women
Are round like fruit. Their encampments are loud
With the bleating of children. They multiply, multiply."
A councilor said: "Your divine majesty
Has some immediate danger in mind?" And Pharaoh:
"War. Should there be war
With some alien people, might not these
Aliens in our midst join with our enemies?
Immediate danger. Let danger be always immediate.
It is a sound thesis. Let us defend ourselves
Before we are attacked." And another councilor:
"Your divine majesty's immediate orders?"
"I specify nothing," Pharaoh said. "I say:
Deal wisely with them. Use—immediate wisdom."
So immediate wisdom, in the dust of hooves
And the shine of metal, thundered into the sheep-shearing.
The pipe faltered and the song ceased and the dance,
Israelite mouths open in wonder and fear
As the captain in metal looked about him, taking his time,
Picking at length on one: "You. Yes, you. Your name?"
The man drew his wife and son and daughter to him, saying:
"Amram. Of the tribe of Levi." And the captain:
"Pay heed, Amram, of the tribe of Levi. You,
Your wife, your son, your daughter, your beasts and chattels,
All that is yours, these from this day stand confiscate
And are given up to the power of Egypt. In the name of
Horus the god, ruler of the world of the living
And of the dead." He signaled abruptly and
The ravaging began: the soldiers, grinning baaaaaah,

Herding the men and women and children like sheep
While the sheep ran bleating in disorder, foodstores trampled,
Tents fired, garments torn, and Amram cried: "Why? Why?"
And the grinning captain answered: "Immediate wisdom."
Therefore did they set over them taskmasters
To afflict them with their burdens.
And they were set to build for Pharaoh treasure cities,
And the names of the cities were Ra'amses and Pithom.
Amram was surprised, pushed down the dusty street
Of Pithom with wife and family, that the enslavement
Had already gone so far: Israelites
Of other tribes long-settled, ready to laugh
At a wavering old man, a newcomer, who cried out:
"You can't cram us in here like so many
Dates in a jar. We're shepherds. We live on the
Open plains. Shut us up here and we'll die—"
"Oh no, not die," jabbed a soldier. "Work, you'll work."
Work, and a whip cracked. The quarters were overcrowded,
Suitable for slaves. Amram at the door, shy, said:
"Jochebed, my wife, and my son Aaron and
Miriam my daughter, and I am Amram of the
Tribe of Levi." A woman said: "Woman of the
Tribe of Levi, help me to help yourselves to a
Little space. A very little." A blind old man
Groped through the noise and smells and dark towards Amram:
"Ah, a good fresh smell of shepherd. Share this
Bit of bread with me, take it, go on. I'd say
That Egyptian food is good food, not that I
See much of it, not that I
See much. Near-blind and old, no good as a worker.
The workers get all. Where are you from then?"
Amram: "From the vale of Shefru." —"I'd say you were a
Liar. I'd say the tribe of Levi was
Never in Shefru." And Amram, patiently:
"My father was Cheat, my father's father was Levi.
Do you follow me? My father's father was
Levi the son of Jacob." And the old man: "I'd
Say that was a possible story. Me and my family,
We're from the tribe of Gad. But you'll find a

Lot of the tribes all mashed together here—
Benjamin, Reuben, Zebulon—a lot of tribes and
All slaves. I'd say there was a sort of mystery in it,
The twelve tribes brought together at last. But in
Slavery, as it's called. I'd say that he was
Laughing at us, it, if he exists that is, you know, the
Old one, older than me, the
God of Abraham, as they call him." Where the children
        were playing
There was a cry and a rattling of little stones
On the clay floor: Miriam, daughter of Amram,
Had pulled a necklace from the neck of an
Older girl, crying: "It's sinful. To wear a thing like that.
An Egyptian thing." Tears and reproaches and the
Mothers and fathers stepping in, but Aaron grinned.
"Grin, then," cried Miriam. "Grin in your slavery.
But he—" And she ran to her mother, putting her head
To her mother's belly to hear the heartbeat within.
"He would not grin, he—" A woman nodded and said:
"So that's the way of it. I wondered." And Jochebed:
"I thought he would be born in Tabris, in the pastures.
We would have been there in three fullnesses of the moon,
At the feast of Nisim." —"*He*, you said. You seem sure."
And the blind old man: "All babies are called
He before they're born. And some of them
Afterwards too." He did not understand the laughter,
Turning his open mouth, like an eye, to the laughter.
Laughter in a place of slaves but in the place of
Royal divinity no laughter. Aromatic oil lamps,
Shadows, effigies, effigies, a cross-legged scribe
Reading to the Pharaoh, Pharaoh cutting in to say:
"The sons of the men of the sand. The name diminishes them.
But they are not diminished." Dutiful smiles
From the assembled councilors. "Continue reading."
"Majesty. *They came from the land of Canaan,
Driven by famine and plague. In Egypt sought they
Grain and pasture, and behold they found them both.
Their sons and their sons' sons grow fat and
Multiply in the houses of the lord of the house of*

Life, the house of death. They multiply and are become
An immense multitude. In order that they may not,
In the event of war, unite with our enemies . . ."
The sentence unfinished, the stylus poised. Pharaoh:
"So it is written, so shall our
Posterity read it. But the sentence is unfinished,
The stylus poised. Let me hear," and he looked at them,
      "wisdom."
There was a pause. The head councilor said:
"This present mode of oppression is clearly
Inefficacious. As I see it, the tribes of Israel,
Mingled together in slavery as they now are,
Lose each its special code of law and restraint.
Constrained from above, they are grown loose beneath.
Lechery, adultery, incest. They grow loose.
They grow. This zest for breeding—it is the mark of
An animal race. They couple like dogs of the desert."
But the Pharaoh said, and they had to strain to hear him:
"And we—we glory in stability, changelessness, power.
Along comes the god of death and says: 'Behold,
I am all these things.' The sentence stands unfinished.
Let the sentence now be pronounced." The poised stylus
Dove to the tablet. "Every son that is born
Shall be cast into the river. But every daughter
Shall be saved alive." The scribe looked up at that.
So it was rods and whips and the occasional
Salutary thrust of the spear that held them back,
The wailing and cursing, as the farm carts filled
With wailing babies. It became a game,
On Nile bank, to see who could throw the farthest,
Bets laid, but some of the soldiers were sick,
And not only on a won bet of a jar of palm wine.
They're *things*, man, no more, go on, *throw*. They threw.
It was a long business. General commanding commanded
A free day and an extra beer ration. They threw,
Some of them, in their sleep. And then calm,
Nile unperturbed, birdsong, a gorgeous day
As the princes came down to the river, a cortège

Of priests intoning:

> Lord of the river and of that quickening mud
> Whence all manner of lowly things are brought to birth,
> Bring to thy servant the gift of fecundity,
> That she may not be despised among the daughters of earth,
> And the worth of her birth be matched by the worth of
>   thy gift.
> Lift her, O river lord, to the ranks of the mothers.

The ritual disrobing: the golden headpiece lifted
To disclose a painful baldness, then the silks
Whistling away from scars, emaciation
On slenderness otherwise comely, framed in
Palms and stonework, royalty unimpaired
By the absurd daubing of Nile mud, the carven
Beauty of the face unmoved, unmoved still
As the filthy rite proceeded, ended, the silks
Were laid to the ulcered flesh, the golden headpiece
Restored, and, to a wordless chant with the rising
Notes of hope in it, the cortège left the river.
The river flowed clear, save for lotus and riverweed,
But then the first of the infant corpses appeared,
Floating downstream.   There had been no craft,
Or perhaps cruelty had its limit, to snatch out the fetus
And examine its sex. So Jochebed came to her time,
Groaning in their corner of a hovel of heavy sleep,
And Amram kneeling anxious by her, each cry of her pain
Forcing him to try to stifle it with his hand:
"Forgive me, my love. Forgive me. Someone may hear.
I trust no one." And some of the sleepers stirred,
Dreaming perhaps of a dead son, then resettled.
One of the sleepers awoke and came softly to him,
And he started, but it was his daughter Miriam.
"There is a sort of shed a little way off,
Full of mattocks and brick molds. It must be there."
He nodded. It was a heavy task, under the moon, dogs baying.
The deformed door creaked. "A space under that cart."
Her agony mounted, Miriam looked wide-eyed, and then
He came out on the flood, crying to the world. As in response

The feet of a patrol could be heard on cobbles
Not too far off, soldiers marching in moonlight
And that cry going out, moonlight flooding his sex.
Sing Miriam prayed and, as in response,
The soldiers sang, and the dirty song was a blessing:

> Here's the way
> We earn our pay
> Who's the enemy we slay?
> Baby Israelites if they
> Have . . .
> That's no way
> To earn your pay
> We would rather any day
> Take their mothers and then lay
> Our . . .

Amram in wonder held the howling child in his arms,
In agony and joy for a second son. And yet, how, how—
"None comes here," Miriam said. "I know. And if any comes,
I shall be in the way of his coming. It must be three
Roundings of the moon. I shall sit here and guard
And I shall weave." Weave? She wove out of bulrushes
And parried queries in the sun. *But where did she go?*
To the house of a cousin, just north of Pithom.
And when will she return? She still has fever.
She sends greeting but begs that none come near her.
The faver is catching. *What is that thing you weave?*
A basket. A cage. A cage for doves. *A cage indeed.*
A cage within a cage. When the cage was finished,
Miriam took it, eager-eyed, to her mother
And the three-month child, milk bubbling on his lip,
And said: "Listen." And Jochebed listened in wonder.
But it was in fear, in working daylight, that Miriam
Carried her cradle or ark to the Nile, opening it
Often and often as she sped through the meadows
To cluck at the child, to whisper "Can you breathe?"
The river's weedy length no longer carried
Human corpses. Rats swam, a fish smote the surface and snapped.
And then a cage of bones, a child's bones. She wept,
Heard an ass bray, started, then was able to smile,

Then to laugh. "Be brave," she whispered. "You have much
    to do."
The baby cried and she hushed him. Then a voice asked:
"What have you in there?" A man's voice. From her crouch
She saw strong legs, hair, leather, a countryman
With a bag and a leather bottle, the face stupid
But not unkind. "My things," she said. "My treasure."
He laughed, and the ass brayed, and the laughter of ladies
Could now be heard, downstream. "Treasure," he braved,
Moving off, then whistled a dog. She, from the reeds,
Watched covertly. Downstream, ladies playing at ball.
And then a deep drum from within the
Palace gardens, it must be, and a male chant
As of some holy procession coming. The ladies quietened,
Made *moues* at each other, then scattered through green.
Then Miriam saw a lady immensely tall,
A gold headpiece, silks liquid in the sun,
Well-attended, languid priestesses, they must be,
And burly priests, coming slowly to the river, intoning:

> You who nourish the reed and tarmarind,
> The date palm and the pepper tree,
> From whose mud the crocodile breeds,
> Many-toothed, tough as a chariot . . .

And it was at that moment that Miriam saw a child's corpse,
Ravaged by rats, float drunkenly downstream. It was the
Moment of courage, to answer the dead with the living,
And she delicately consigned the bulrush cage or cradle
To the waters. The princess, she must be, said, seeing
In revulsion that bloated and bitten cadaver,
"You address the river as a river of life. Leave me."
They waited, unsure. "Leave me, leave me." And they left,
Save for her, it must be, waiting-woman, maid.
"Live," whispered Miriam, "live." A current took the
Cage, cradle, ark and swirled it shoreward,
Into the reeds. The lady saw. The ladies saw. The
Princess, it must be, said: "That. What is it? Go in and
Bring it to me. Quick, before the river
Takes it again." And it was so. To what or whom,

Miriam wondered, did one pray now? She prayed to the
Infant now passing from arms to arms, yelling hard
Against the melting wall of surprise: *Let them that would kill
Preserve and nourish. More. The royal river
Gives you to a royal house. A prince in Egypt.
Joseph was a prince in Egypt.* They were lost in green,
The child's crying, the ladies cooing. Miriam's task
Was not yet done. She left the river. In the royal garden
A twitter of ladies (who is he where is he from well-fed
Look at those ringlets of fat why is he here who is his
Mother the Nile is his father anyway) about the arms of the
Princess, hushing him, saying to him not to cry, singing:

> Out of the desert the wind blows strong
> But cool but cool from out of the sea
> The desert burns and the day is long . . .

"He is hungry." She stopped, they turned to the source
            of the voice,
Miriam standing boldly at the fringe of the garden,
An empty vase in her hands (a servant to get flowers,
No questions asked). "He is good. He only cries
When he is hungry." And then the flurry of who are you
Who let you in here call the guards. But the princess:
"Wait." They desisted. "Come here, girl." She came,
Uneasy but without deference. "You know this child?"
Miriam: "I am an Israelite. We know no
Men children. The Egyptians kill them at birth."
"How do you know this child is a boy?" No answer.
"Do you know his mother?" And Miriam said boldly:
"I know many mothers who weep for their sons. Whose
Breasts are heavy with milk." And the princess:
"You mean you can find me a nurse among the Israelites?"
"Yes. One who weeps and whose
Breasts are heavy with milk." The princess was eager:
"Bring her. For my son. For he is my son.
And his father is the Nile. His name shall be
Moses. Meaning *my son.*" But Miriam, full of light, said:
"Meaning, in our tongue: *I have brought him forth.*"
And she sped back to Pithom for Jochebed. A royal summons.

The eyes of the other women narrowed. Why? What?
What is this about? Saying more, seeing
Daughter and mother leave and the mother, fevered so long,
So heavy-breasted. But the princess said
(And Jochebed had no eyes for the garden, the marble,
Effigies, effigies, only for the one she suckled):
"What is your name?"
"Does your breast hurt you?"
"I am sorry that your little boy
Died." But Miriam, bold, said: "Was killed."
And the princess: "We—mothers cannot easily understand
High state policy. We are the givers of life,
Daughters of the sun. Men turn their backs on the sun
To build labyrinths out of the light. The labyrinths
Breed strange monsters. These become the
Gods of darkness. Men love their dark gods."
The ladies looked at her strangely. Heresy? The leavings of
Some ancient faith, destroyed because inconvenient,
Hence heresy? But the princess said to Jochebed:
"You will come back. In four hours' time.
And you will keep coming back until he has
No further need of you. When he has done with your breast,
He shall be wholly mine. You will forget him.
Entirely. Completely. Forever. My son.
You will be paid, of course. One of you, pay her."
A coin in her unwilling hand, a coin in
Amram's hand, a gold coin in Pithom. And the women said:
"She sold her child to the Egyptians. To save him.
Why should her child be saved and none of ours?
Cunning. What is so special about her son that
He could be saved? She sold her child for
Money. Whores sell their children,
Whores." A man said *whore* at Jochebed,
And she said nothing. Another spat in her path.
Amram said nothing. And then he said, to Jochebed:
"What name have they given him?" She shrugged, saying:
"Moses." *Moses.* Amram tasted the name,
Not liking it much. It was not the name
That he would have given the boy. Miriam said, full of light:

"Meaning, in our tongue, *I have brought him forth.*"
They looked at her strangely, a strange girl, full of
Strange imaginings, not like other girls. Moses, then.
Mouths round on the name, they went in to supper.
Corn mash, garlic, dates, beer. A gold coin
Useless in Pithom. *I have brought him forth.*

2 | THE YOUNG MOSES

AND she whom he called mother came to die.
During dalliance in a royal garden, close to sunset,
He thought he heard, raising his lips from the
Offered lips to listen. The girl teased:
"You hear bats. You hear field mice. You hear locusts.
But you always hear them at the wrong time—"
"I thought," he said, "I heard," frowning, "my mother—"
"*My mother*," in mockery gentle enough, and she tried to
Pull his mouth down to hers, he resisted, she pouted.
He rose and ran, she running after, laughing,
Through green mazes, reaching cool stone, effigies,
Effigies, the palace of the princess. The princess
Lay in cool gloom, a jewel, muted by the gloom,
In a bone cage that had been hands, her voice muted,
Saying: "Give this to her, send her away, you will have
Many jewels, many girls to give them to. But tonight
There is one girl who must say, must say:
Where is my lord? I am taken from him. She is
Lingering outside. I can smell desire and life.
Take it to her." So he took it to where she waited,
Plump among the effigies, and she snatched it, saying:
"What is it worth?" And he: "If it were worth all the
Gold of the king's," smiling, "gold mines—"
"I know, I know, it could not be so precious
As our night together. Which we shall not have."
Pouting, then smiling, fingering her jewel.
"I shall be hungry tonight for your hands." Thinking **already**

Of other hands, but then only of his hands,
For there were no hands like his in all Egypt.
He left her, taking those hands to the mother's body,
Hands of a healer, saying as he kneaded kneaded
Gently: "The body. Is a mystery. Like the heavens.
If we could turn for a moment. The skin.
The flesh. To glass. Then we could see the.
Wonders of the streets. Of the city within.
The streets are sometimes roaring. With evil invaders.
Then we talk. Of a sickness. Here are two roads.
That lead to the. Citadel of your lungs. If I could
Clear those. Infested ways. You would be
Well again." And she said, lulled: "They tell me
That you love wisdom, but not all the time. Your senses
Get in the way of thought. You hear bats and field mice
Crying. They say that you become impatient."
And Moses, rapt in the office his hands performed:
"Impatient. Sometimes. They say that the
Wisdom of Egypt is. Complete and sealed. That there is
No new wisdom. To be learned. The death of a
Man. Means more than the. Birth of a. Child.
For what new wisdom. Can the. Child bring to the
World? Egypt looks to the. End. The closure. The
Seal." And she: "You do not see things as an
Egyptian does, as a true Egyptian does. They want
Certainty. Death is all too certain—"
"If it is so. Certain why is it not. More simple?
It is expressed through. So many gods. Hawk-faced.
Dog-headed. Crocodile-toothed. It is a. Darkness.
Full of monsters." And she: "When I was a girl,
I remember, there were men who taught a simple faith.
A faith of the sun, which it seemed right to worship,
The lifegiver. The men were heard for a time,
Then soon not even heard of." And he, half to himself,
Lulled by his own hands' ministry: "The wise men.
Have taught me to see. Beauty in the many. Beautiful.
Death in the many. Forms of death. Could there not be a.
Light that is not. The sun. But which the sun. Uses?"
She then, urgent: "Give me light, Moses. Light the torches."

"But," he said, "the sun is not yet down."
"Light them just the same. I fear the dark.
I would go to the sun and be consumed in him.
But soon there will be no sun." So he lighted them,
And she said: "You came from the water. I must return to it.
Embark on a boat whose pennant is the sun that shines
        in the dark.
Whose name is the name of the god of the harvest of souls.
Whose oars are the arms of a god whose face I must not see.
And the keel of the boat is truth. Or justice.
I am ferried to the western bank of the river,
For there the sun has his setting. And there I
Find a secret way into the earth.
I am going to the river. And you
Were brought out of the river. The same river?"
So Moses, with troubled affection, stroked her brow,
But the hands had no magic . . .
                                A grain city,
In wood and baked clay and wire, a toy for Mernefta,
Crown prince of Egypt, cousin to Moses, only a child
But imperious enough, filled the chamber and he strode over it,
Seeing the whole city from his sky like a god, while a
Chamberlain pointed out this and this, not quite a toy then
But a projected glory of the empire, a torment for slaves.
Moses came and said: "You summoned me, my lord."
And the boy: "It is *highness* you must call me, cousin.
Your highness. I have searched for you all day
And everywhere. That is not right." ("Not right.
Your highness." "You promised to take me to hunt
Crocodiles." Deferential, a little amused, said:
"Ah yes, your highness. But then. I reconsidered.
Your highness. What would have happened to me.
If the crocodiles had. Snapped and eaten you?
What would have happened. To the throne of. Egypt?"
A child's scowl: "You, I suppose, would have taken it.
I am angry with you, cousin." A little amused, sad:
"Do not be angry. Your highness. Not now. I am come.
To tell you sad news." Then the chamberlain, a man's scowl:
"His highness is not to be given sad news. That is laid down."

Moses, ignoring him: "My mother is dead. Your
Father's sister. The Princess Bithiah.
Is dead." A child's cruelty: "Dead? Like the
Three thousand men who built the treasure city,
And the ones who will die building this? "Hitting it.
"Yes. Highness. There is only. One way of being
Dead." But the child was more than a child: "No.
Those dead will be forgotten. Not one name
Of one of them will be rembered. But
My name will be written there. They will take hammers
And hammer my name into stone. Mernefta,
Fifth king of his dynasty, first of them all for glory.
And the thousands of dead, five or six thousand,
Forgotten. A fine thing." The chamberlain, impatient:
"Highness, you have forgotten the purpose
For which your cousin was sent here." And the boy: "Ah, yes.
You, cousin, are to go and see the workers.
To see that they are building right. I asked my father
That you be sent. It is a punishment, you see.
You should have taken me hunting." A little amused, sad,
Bowing: "As your highness says. A punishment."
But there was a task to perform first. Among the effigies,
In the reek of the holy fires, he stood, watching,
While, with wands of obsidian, the priests and priestesses
Opened her dead eyes and mouth, intoning:

> Your lips I open in the god's name,
> That you may speak and eat.
> Your eyes I open in the god's name,
> That light and sight may bless them.
> But not the gross tastes and speech of the earth.
> But not the insubstantial light of the sun
> That warms the earth. When you awaken
> And depart from the tomb, at the endless
> End of the sacred river underground,
> You will raise your eyes to light eternal,
> Open your mouth in speech
> That is soundless since it is the soul of speech.
> Let all my offenses be forgotten dust.
> Let tribulation be as motes in the sun

When the sun is down.
Greetings to you, greatest god of the underworld.
At length my eyes are brought to the
Witness of your beauty, whose eternal contemplation
Is my sole care. I know your name at last,
As I know the names of the two and forty gods
Who preside in the halls of the eternal.
I am become one to whom sin is not even a name.
I am become one who had no eyes for his false path.

And line by coil the winding sheet rose to the
Neck, the mouth, the nostrils. The eyes alone
Were uncovered. So Moses took the linen, trembling,
And covered them, saying: "You who became my mother
Out of your goodness
Who leave me motherless
And yet with a mother
Still to be sought,
Farewell." And the ceremony was ended. It was time to
Engage the sun, the living and dying, not the dead. Duty.
Officers of the court invested him in the
Traveling robes of a prince. A princely horse,
With jeweled caparison, pawed dust out of the earth.
He mounted, was saluted, rode off with officers,
Attendants, a body-servant, towards Pithom, asking:
"Pithom. And what is the life of Pithom?"
"Slaves, your highness. But sometimes unruly. Enslaved,
But a stubborn people. A very alien people."
Dust and sun and travel. Birds screaming.
But, in a hovel in Pithom, a woman screaming.
The workers passed to work, shrugging, an Egyptian
Overseer claiming his rights from a woman of Israel,
Wife of a slave, what could they do? Still—*cuckold*.
Always a hard word. But what could the cuckold do?
The cuckold, Dathan, inclining to the side of the rulers,
Hence a foreman of workers, opened his own door
To see himself being cuckolded. Inclining to the side
Of the rulers, but showing truculence. The overseer
Looked up, grinning, from the bed, the frightened wife,
To say: "You should not be here, should you, Dathan?"

"It seems not," said Dathan, "but I have certain rights—"
"No rights, Dathan." —"Not even the right
To report to my superior official? Officially?"
Grinning, "Not even that right. You will report
When you are officially ordered to report. In the meantime,
You have duties to carry out." And Dathan, truculent:
"Duties to my own manhood." The Egyptian laughed at that,
And rose from Dathan's bed, though lazily, saying:
"Only free men can talk of manhood. What does Dathan
The unfree have to say?" And the unfree: "Straw.
The straw has not arrived." The overseer: "Oh,
Use some of your own. Man of straw." The hands of Dathan,
As of their own will, were on to the ravisher,
Slid, sweating, on his tunic near the neck. Teeth gritted.
Teeth grinned: "An example, little Dathan.
An example is required. Would you not say so? An example."
On the worksite, where the Israelites slapped mud into
        brick forms,
All eyes looked up in a sort of relief (relief at the prospect of
Change in any shape, even change for the worse)
At arriving hooves. Gold, snorting horses, Egyptians.
Whips cracked, work you dogs and so on, they were
        used to whips.
Miriam the woman was bringing water in a jar. She, too,
        looked up
And her brother Aaron, a man now, or slave, drinking, too,
Looked up at an unknown voice. An Egyptian prince
But not quite an Egyptian, the voice hopping like a bird
Not clanking like endless metal: "Is not this man
Too ill to work?" And an officer, idly swishing a fly fan;
"He is not too ill to work if he is still working."
And the prince saw, frowning, the lashed back of another,
Asking: "What is this?" And the worker replied:
"It is what might be termed an inducement to increased effort—"
"You speak like a scholar. Are you a scholar?"
"I was a scholar of sorts. When scholarship was allowed."
Aaron and Miriam looked at each other. Was it not perhaps
Just possible that— The prince said: "Their quarters.
I will see their. No. Alone. I will go alone." So it was

That, alone on the Pithom street between the hovels,
The women looking up curious, the children following,
Moses heard pain and the crunch of a rod. He opened a door
On to a naked man held by two men, grinning, Israelites
All three, and a sweating overseer, panting, punishing,
The man howling, a woman sobbing on a bed. The overseer,
Seeing an Egyptian aristocrat come in, smirked
With an air of virtue and smote hard: Dathan howled.
Moses cried: "Stop. What is this?" Paused, panting, saying:
"Punishment. My lord. For inefficiency. For insolence.
For insubordination." And raised the rod. Dathan: "For
Not. Wanting. To be a." The rod fell, he howled. Moses:
"You. Assistants. Are Israelites?" And the overseer panted:
"They are Israelites, my lord. This is their foreman.
They naturally have no love for their foreman. Now.
If you will permit me." And he raised, and the hand of Moses,
To the surprise of Moses, rose and grasped the rod,
And the mouth of Moses, to the surprise of Moses, said:
"I gave an order. I said *stop*. I call that also
Insolence. Insubordination." And Moses, to the surprise
Not only of Moses, leapt from a rock into a
Gorgeous sea of anger, beating beating, following the
Crawling stupefied beaten about the floor, beating.
The Israelites watched with pleasure different from
Their former pleasure, Dathan bled in pleasure but
Shock crowned the pleasure: this surely was what was the word
This was insanity. Without the door women listened,
Children, old men, young men coming off shift,
Screams and beating but soon no more of either,
Only breath sharply intaken and a desperate sobbing
For breath from one. And, within, that one
Dropped the rod, looked narrowly, saw then about him
Eyes not narrow at all, the woman's eyes especially
Wide in incredulity, then found breath to, to his surprise,
Excuse the beast that had possessed and was now departing:
"It was. Too much. But a. Man does not.
Die of a beating. His heart stopped. His heart
Suddenly stopped." And Dathan, to the two
Who had held him: "My time will come for you. Friends.

Now back to work. This is none of your concern."
They shuffled. "I have things to remember, have I not?
Bloody things."
        Quick to leave, leaving the door wide,
Shocked faces to look in, elation, fear, feelings
Not easily definable. Dathan: "You killed him, you.
You will go away and say that I did it.
They will all say that I did it." But Moses, calm now:
"No one killed him. His heart suddenly stopped.
But the. Responsibility. Is mine." And then, addressing
      the clamor:
"You see a dead Egyptian in your midst.
But you have no cause. For fear. The
Blame will not. Be visited on you. He was
Killed by his own. Brutality. His heart burst.
Have no fear." An old man, near-blind, said: "I'd say that
It was a strange thing to hear an Egyptian lord
Speak against brutality. Who are you, young man, who
Speak of Egyptian brutality?" And at last in Pithom
It was heard aloud at last: "My name is Moses."
And he thrust through them, man of authority, yet drawn
In a way he could not yet explain to himself
To these vigorous slaves. *Moses.* The crowd handled it,
Rang it like a coin, tasted it, the corpse bloody on the floor,
The killer at large, the police pushing in: Who did it?
Who saw? I saw, I saw, his name is Moses. The prince Moses?
This is nonsense, an Egyptian slaying an Egyptian
In the presence of slaves. But, in her father's house,
Miriam, ecstatic, spoke: "Moses. It has come true."
Aaron, far from ecstatic, carper and doubter,
Said: "Nothing has come true. Except that
What seems to you a beginning is really an end.
All Pithom talks of him already as if he were
Already the deliverer. You have kept his name
Alive on their lips, though in a whisper, these twenty years.
So now he is an Israelite who has killed an Egyptian.
There is no promise of anything save further servitude.
We must go on groveling to Egyptian gods for, believe me,
Those gods prevail and will always prevail." Amram, old now,

Said: "The voice is the voice of a prophet, my son,
But the words are a slave's words." Wild-eyed, Aaron:
"I see things as they are. I am not, like my sister here,
Wild-eyed." And Jochebed the old woman: "When he,
When he walks into this house—" Aaron: "If, if.
He must leave, or else be a sacrifice to Egypt.
He will have no time for walking into houses."
But she: "When he walks into the house of his parents,
I shall be expected to have words, but what words
I do not know. I loved a child I lost.
And now I must expect the pain of learning to
Love a child who is found. And must be lost again."
But Moses, walking alone, touching and smelling this
Alien race, finding it not alien, exerting authority
That did not seem to him that of an alien, came to a place
Where one Israelite fought another, both bloody from fists,
With a divided crowd making cockfight noises,
And cried "Stop this" so that they stopped an instant,
But only that one of the fighters could pant out: "Ah,
The Lord Moses. Are you come then to be our judge?
To strike us down as you struck the Egyptian down?"
And Moses said nothing but felt the tremor of the
Fear of the hunted, wondering why. "Moses," the jeer went,
"Our judge and our executioner?" A boy in the crowd
Came to Moses and tugged at the princely robe
And spoke and Moses bent to hear, not understanding,
Not at all well understanding, not at first.
But Dathan, blood washed off, bruised, limping,
But in his best robe, understood well enough,
Going from man to man in authority,
Telling his story: "I have served well, sir, my lord,
And it is my ambition to serve better.
I would not utter the dirty word *payment*, of course—"
You will be paid whatever your information
Is worth. Do not waste time.
"I had thought of, perhaps, some small promotion."
Do not waste time. "Waste time, no. I have witnesses
Outside to testify to the murder of our overseer,
A good just man. A senseless murder, if I may say so."

Do not. "The Lord Moses was the slayer."
He had authority to exert discipline. Go on.
"The Lord Moses, with respect, sir, had no such authority.
He is an Israelite. The Princess Bithiah
(May her soul have rest) took him out of the Nile.
It is a long story which I will be happy to tell.
He is the son of Jochebed and Amram of the tribe of Levi.
He was saved by his sister in the old time of the
Necessary execution of the children." And then,
Not liking the silence, "I tell no lie. Sir, my lord,
Gentlemen, I tell no lie." But the silence was the
Silence of rumination of the delectable bread of
Coming intrigue. There were some who hated Moses.
Something un-Egyptian about him. Bastard spewed by the river.
Stories, stories. "I tell no lie." *Give him some*
Bauble or other. Tell him to wait outside.
And the boy from the crowd led Moses to Miriam,
By a tree near the house of Amram. Miriam spoke,
Moses listened, things coming clear, though in pain.
"You believe?" she asked. "Believe?" He said: "I was told
Of a taking from the water. My mother. As I
Called her. Hid nothing. Save for names. And names
She did not know. Perhaps not. Wishing to know.
Said that I was nourished. On Israelite milk. That a
Girl of the Israelites. Found me my nurse." And Miriam:
"I know the palace, can describe the chamber,
The gardens. There was an inscription said,
Or they said it said, he was to be born in the
House of the king, but a lady said that every
House in Egypt was a house of the king." Moses: "Who?
Who?" She said: "He who was to come, the child of the
Sun they called him. But to me he was to be
More than the child of the sun. Will you come home?"
"You mean," he said, "I am to. Find a mother?"
Miriam said: "You are to find a family."
Torches, horsemen, heralds positioning themselves
Among public effigies, effigies, the political men at work,
The trumpet and then the proclamation:
"Be it known that Moses the Israelite,

ANTHONY BURGESS

Once falsely known as the Lord Moses,
Stands accused of the murder of a
Servant of the king, a free man, an Egyptian.
Let him be rendered up to authority.
Any who hide him or otherwise grant comfort
Render themselves liable to the exaction of the
Capital penalty. So written, so uttered."
So the time for shy discovery in the house of Amram,
For the turning of an Israelite into an Israelite,
Was not long. The fine Egyptian silks
Were stuffed in a hollow in the wall, lidded with a stone,
And the Lord Moses was turned into an Israelite,
In a worn gray cloak, with the wanderer's staff
In hands that were not yet hands of an Israelite.
He smiled. "I will learn to be an Israelite.
But not in. Slavery. In exile rather. Not a
Slave. Merely a. Fugitive." They wept. Miriam said:
"We shall be together in the time of the setting free."
But Aaron, bitterly: "If ever such a time should come."
But Moses, not yet understanding: "In the time of the."
The time that stretched now was the time of understanding,
Trying to learn to understand. With the sun setting,
He set his face to the desert. *Be it known that
Moses the Israelite.* Set his face to the desert.

3 | THE BURNING BUSH

IT was not, he thought, if it could be called thought,
This shuffling or churning in his skull,
That the desert was empty. The desert was not empty,
Far far from empty: it was a most intricate poem
On the theme of thirst and hunger, it was a
Crammed gallery of images of himself, suffering,
And it rang with songs that never got beyond
The opening phrase, like: *Went to find an Israelite*
And found himself athirst or *I am baked meat*
I cannot eat. Once in joy he contended with
The collective appetite of a million flies
Over a migratory quail, almost fleshless, fallen in flight.
Twice he found porous rock that, struck with his staff
Though feebly, disgorged a fresh trickle. He lapped, blessing,
Though what to bless? There was once stone
That he wished to take for some effigy but a
Thought of last night's stars made him ashamed.
The way of Egypt with the stars was to make them
Bow down to the muddy god of the Nile, but here
They were, in a manner, unmolested. Nor, so it seemed to him,
Was it all straight lines up there, joining star to star,
No Egyptian geometry. Curves rather. Seeing that
Egypt was all measuring-rods, squares, cubes, pyramids,
But Unegypt, which could be, might as well be,
Israel, was curves—fruit and the leaping of lambs
And the roundness of the body gloried in not constrained
In geometry. Was he delirious, hearing himself say

ANTHONY BURGESS

God is round? The term meant nothing except that the
Sun and the moon possessed this perfect roundness,
But one day he saw sun and moon in the morning together
And saw more than that, heard himself saying:
Not one not the other but the light that is given to both.
Given, that was it, but by what given? What or whom?
The god of the, the gods of the. Miriam had talked
Of the God of the Israelites, the God of Jacob.
Again the god of the. And you tamed the stars then
And set them to prophesying mud. God. The stars were back
In their firmament, aloof. Words mean what exists.
God not a word then. A cantrip. A device for
Keeping the stars free. At some uncounted dawn
On whatever day it was he saw ahead a mountain,
Must be a mountain, no mirage, with a nap of green,
But that could be mirage, as could as must be that
Tree in the distance, solitary palm, fronds soon able to be
Counted. Counting, though, was Egyptian arithmetic,
Not apt for the desert. Reality too was royal,
Must be accorded the courtesy of averted eyes,
Not too boldly approached. Tried the cantrip *God*
To hold the tree there, and it held. Too weak to hurry, though.
The song of the daughters he could not yet hear,
Was a real song, royal, more than a first line:

> What will love bring
> When he comes?
> A silver ring.
> Earth will ring
> With his tread
> When he comes.
> On his head
> A kingly crown
> When he comes down
> From the hill.
> What will he bring?
> A silver ring
> When he comes . . .

The mountain had a name: Horeb. This was tree-grown pasture
In a valley, and from the well at dawn

Jethro's daughters drew, singing. But the song stopped
When the leering shepherds arrived, pushing in
        with their buckets,
With *Away from there, bitches, find another well,*
Scratch, would you, if you want to scratch
Scratch this itch. Then he came down from the hill,
Wearing dust not silver, crowned with his second anger,
His staff held high, then he smote like a king,
But after fell for faintness, seeing them run
And calling *Mad mad, he is mad,* leaving blood in the dust.
Surrounded by round-armed girls, he smiled then
Turned up his eyes, seeing round flesh and green
And after nothing but ringing indistinguishable
Suns and moons. But he awoke in a tent smelling
Sheep's cheese, sheep's milk, new bread, an old shepherd
Smiling over him, a girl named Zipporah
Solicitous with a bowl, bread torn into warm milk.
He ate and gave his name, a man cast out of Egypt,
Seeking a new life. Jethro, set around with girls,
Was all too ready to talk to a man, talked at length:
"I was once a priest of the town of Midian.
But I grew sick of stone idols, grew to believe
That faith was concerned with—well, not with,
If you know the word, multiplicity. A man
Must worship something great and simple. In the desert
Sometimes one sees an image of this. On Mount Horeb, there
A man, I sometimes think, might see an even greater
Image of the truth. Out of meditation.
I have seen no visions. Perhaps I am too old.
I am certainly too old to climb it." Zipporah,
Gently: "Come to our story, father." Jethro smiled,
Saying: "Yes yes, I wander. It is easily told.
I turned against idols, the people against me.
We are cut off. My daughters must draw water
Before the Midian shepherds leave their beds,
Otherwise they may draw no water. But they come
Earlier and earlier. Depriving us of water
Has become a cruel sport. I am grateful for what you did."
Moses: "You have said that. Many times. Already."

But Zipporah: "Gratitude is not a word.
It is the desire to keep on saying the word."
"My daughters," Jethro said, "are forward in their speech,
If not in their deeds. How can one man prevail
Against so many women?" Then, after a pause:
"You are traveling farther? Perhaps to the town itself?"
Moses said: "For the moment. My own story.
Ends here. My journey has been. Into exile.
For exile is everywhere. For the exile."
Jethro asked: "Can you do shepherd's work?"
Moses said: "I had always been taught. That work.
Was for slaves. Egypt taught me. Many false things."
Jethro, urgently: "Put off that word *exile*.
It is your people who know exile, not you." And Moses, softly:
"Yes. I must learn. To think of them. As my people."
My people, lashed to labor under the disdainful eyes
Of a growing prince, and Moses already growing
Into a myth. The time would soon come in Pithom
For a story told by the old to the young: "Moses.
That was his name. He was brought up a royal prince
But one day he turned against the Egyptians. He
Killed some of them. Oh, I do not know how many,
But there were certainly many. He was strong, you see,
Like a bull or a lion. Yes yes, or a crocodile.
And then he escaped out of Egypt for they wished to kill him.
Some say he will come back. But I believe he is
Dead in the desert, eaten by vultures or something,
Just very white bones now, picked clean.
No no, not eaten by crocodiles, where is your sense?
There are no crocodiles in the desert. It is in the
Water you get crocodiles. They are full of water.
Their eyes are full of water. They cry when they eat you."
Then the old king died and the prince Mernefta
Ruled in his turn, the new Pharaoh, remembering Moses,
But not yet as a myth. "His accusers," he said one day.
"Are any of these still living?" And a minister:
"Majesty, the accusation was naturally
Brought by the Crown. The Crown is still living."
But Pharaoh said: "The Crown is he who wears it.

I hardly need my father's dusty archives
As part of my inheritance. Is there a
Living accuser who does not wear a crown?"
"Some Israelites," was the answer, "who swore that the
Accused was himself an Israelite." Pharaoh rose
And walked his council chamber among effigies, effigies,
Slaves following with fans. "I knew him. Moses. I
Remember him with some tenderness—an elder cousin
Who was always promising to take me hunting.
Crocodiles. I do not believe he liked hunting.
He would listen to bats and the cries of field mice.
No one else would hear them—only he. I cannot
Easily see him as a great vengeful lion, striking
Men dead with a rod." A minister said: "There
Was a death, majesty. An Egyptian corpse. Very bloody."
"Men," said Pharaoh, "are not, I think, beaten to death.
The beater must die of exhaustion first. So. It was
Officially I who sent him to Pithom and to this
Old accusation. Did I also send him
To death in the desert?" Another minister said:
"There is no certainty of his death. At least
Two caravans have brought back news. News of a sort.
Of, for instance, a hero who came out of Egypt
And into Midian, killed twenty men with a blow,
Married seven or eight sisters—the exact number is unclear.
The name we heard seemed to be some
Outlandish deformation of his true name." Pharaoh smiled.
"I would prefer him to be back with us. It would be
Good to see him smiling at my triumphs.
His smile was like none else's—no fanfare of teeth.
It always seemed to hold back, to hold something back."
And the first minister said: "So, majesty,
The sentence is quashed? The accusation canceled?"
Pharaoh said: "Let us have him in Egypt again."
But not even a king of Egypt could put time back.
Moses the shepherd, with his, or Jethro's, flocks,
Dreaming under Horeb, dreamed of no future other than
A shepherd's future. A husband and a father,
His wife, as was to be foreseen, the eldest, Zipporah,

His son named Gershom, strange name, apter for himself:
Stranger in a strange land. And the future? Well—
There was the taking of Jethro's place, when the time came,
And the time could not be long. Problem of girls
Without dowries, a whole family cut off
From the idolators of Midian. He turned now to wave
At Jethro watching him, Zipporah, Gershom in her arms,
Up there by the tents and the palm, rain clouds behind them,
This being a place of rare rain, but of rain.
Jethro was saying to Zipporah: "Now you see how
A good shepherd works. First he takes to pasture
The very young, so that they may eat of the
Tender grass, full of juice, and then the older ones
That they may eat what is fitting for them, and last
The full-grown sheep that can chew the tough grass. All this
I did not teach him: he seemed to know it already."
The child Gershom cried, and Zipporah rocked him,
Singing: "Gershom—Gershom—stranger in a
Strange land." Her father said: "A gloomy lullaby.
A gloomy name. It rings somehow of his father.
Settled and not settled. Never quite at rest.
But a good son-in-law. An only son-in-law."
In sad affection he turned his eyes to the other girls,
Washing clothes and squabbling. A good son-in-law,
Carrying a lamb to the desert for sacrifice,
The knife raised, Jethro intoning: "Unknown of the desert,
Great one, faceless, voiceless, we offer thee this
Fruit of the fertile lands. Accept it of thy goodness,
Eternal unity, whatever, whoever thou art." But the name
Moses, Moisha, Musa was no unknown of the desert.
The Egyptian patrols heard it among nomads, searching,
As they had been bidden, but long in finding.
Until at dawn, waking to birdsong, smiling, he suddenly
Started, and she said: "What do you hear? I hear nothing,
Nothing but birdsong." But he grasped his robe, rising,
And left the tent to see horsemen on the hill crest,
Egyptians. The daughters of Jethro welcomed them,
With yesterday's bread, pitchers of well water,
And their leader spoke to Moses, saying: "You have proof

That this is your name?" Moses smiled and replied:
"A name is merely. What a man is called. I am
Called Moses. My wife is called Zipporah. My son is
Gershom. And here is my. Wife's father. Jethro."
"The documents I hold," said the officer, taking bread
With a desert courtesy, "are signed by the royal hand.
They attest your right to return to Egypt freely,
To resume your former status, former office."
"My status. And office. You see. I am a shepherd.
I am an Israelite." But the leader swallowed and said:
"You are the Lord Moses, cousin to the Pharaoh.
As such, your place and duty are self-evident.
If I may say so. With respect." But Moses said:
"You are not then come. To force me. Back to Egypt?"
"I have no such authority. I am but the bearer
Of a royal message." And Moses spoke his last words to them
(They were welcome to rest. Then let them return to Egypt):
"My compliments. To the Pharaoh. Tell him that I,
Too, have my kingdom." He left them, broke bread alone,
Then led his lambs to pasture. But that day
Was to be no common day. Tending his flocks,
He heard a sound from Horeb, a sound as of the
Manifold cracking of twigs in the fire, and he turned
To see the mountain melting, shifting towards him,
Then setting in its old shape: an illusion
Of a more than Egyptian kind, occasioned no doubt
By today's voices from Egypt. But, peering, he saw
What seemed no magic: there on the upper slope
A flame that burned steady. Who had made fire on Horeb?
He left his lambs and, staff in hand, incredulous,
Moved to the mountain. The flame burned steady.
Its reality was somehow fixed in his brain by the
Smell of wool grease on the hand that he lifted to
Shade his eyes from the light, to see better the
Fame that burned steady on the upper slope. So, slowly,
Driven solely by desire for a strange thing to be
No longer strange, he began to climb, and the climb
Hid the flame from him until, sweating, panting,
No longer a young prince racing over the delta,

He faced at length a boulder on the upper slope
And rounded, panting, the boulder and there he saw a
Flame burning steady but the flame calm as a diamond
And the flame the flame of a bush burning, its leaves
Burning but not consumed, and sound from the flame
As of the noise of some element striving with little skill
To become a voice, then finding more skill and becoming the
Voice of his sister Miriam. "Miriam!" And, in Miriam's voice:
"Come no closer. Put off your shoes from your feet.
For the place whereon you are standing is holy ground."
He was slow to obey. "Miriam? How is it possible?
Miriam?" And the voice: "I speak through the voices
Of those who are near and yet far. The voice of your father."
And the voice was of his father. "Put off your shoes.
For this is holy ground." And Moses, not without trembling,
His fingers clumsy, clumsily obeyed. "I speak also
With your own voice, but a voice no longer
Slow and unassured." And so it was, his own voice,
Saying: "I am the God of your father,
The God of Abraham, the God of Isaac,
The God of Jacob. And also the God of Moses.
Listen. I have surely seen the affliction
Of my people in Egypt, and have heard their cry
By reason of their taskmasters. For I know their sorrows.
And I am come to deliver them out of the hands
Of the Egyptians, and to bring them out of that land
Unto a good land and a large, a land that
Flows with milk and with honey. Now therefore behold:
The cry of the children of Israel is come unto me.
Therefore I will send unto Pharaoh
You, Moses, charged with the task of
Bringing forth my people, the children of Israel,
Out of the land of Egypt." But Moses, hesitant,
Stumbling, in his own voice, what there was of his voice,
Said: "Who am I. That I should. Go to Pharaoh.
And should should. Bring the children. Of Israel.
Out of." But the voice said: "I will be with you,
I. And when you have brought them out of Egypt,
You shall serve God upon this mountain." *God.*

"It is God who sends you. God. The God of your fathers."
But Moses: "And if I say. The God of your fathers
Has sent me to you. And they say. What is his name?
What shall I. Say to them?" And the voice replied:
"You shall say to the children of Israel what he is called,
For what he is called he is: I am that I am.
And say too: the Lord God of your fathers,
The God of Abraham, the God of Isaac,
The God of Jacob has sent me unto you. And I am sure
That the king of Egypt will not let you go,
No, not by a mighty hand. But I will stretch out
My hand, my, and smite Egypt with all my wonders."
Moses said: "But they will. Not believe me. They will
Say: the Lord has. Not appeared unto you."
But the voice: "What is that in your hand?" And Moses:
"My shepherd's staff."—"Cast it to the ground."
And Moses, bewildered, did so, and the staff,
Touching the ground, writhed, hissed, a snake.
A snake. He started back, afraid. And the voice said:
"Put out your hand. Take it by the tail."
And Moses did so, still afraid, and what he took
Was his own shepherd's staff, no snake. Then the voice said:
"Through this power they will believe. And through this too:
Put your hand into your bosom." Moses slowly did so,
Doubtful still. "Now remove it." Did so, and his hand
Was white with leprosy. "Return it your bosom,
Then remove it." Did so, and the hand was of its
Former color. "If," said the voice, "they will not
Believe one sign, then let them believe the other."
Moses, now near weeping, said: "O Lord. I am not
Eloquent. Not before. Not now. I am
Slow of speech. I am of a. Slow tongue."
The voice was thunder, crying in fire and thunder:
"Who has made man's mouth?
Who made the dumb or deaf or the seeing or the blind?
Am I not the Lord? For a time, for a time,
Your brother Aaron shall speak for you, and you
Shall put the staff in his hand. But with you, with you
Shall be the power of the Lord." And the bush burned

But was silent. Burned still, the leaves and branches
Still unconsumed. He believed, he had to believe,
Believed, had to believe, descending to his sheep,
To the evening fire, the meat roasting, to Jethro saying:
"You believe that you saw what you saw, heard what
        you heard?"
Believed, had to believe. "And thus a heavy burden
Is placed upon you. So." Seeing it all. "It is true.
The one. The great simplicity. The is what he is.
Well, at least I can die in the truth, knowing it the truth.
But for you a heavy burden." Moses, sighing:
"My shoulders are too narrow. My voice is not the. Voice.
Of a deliverer. Easier to believe. It was a dream.
It was a whiff of magic. Delivered out of Egypt."
His head fell to his bosom in a sudden sleep.
Zipporah started but Jethro shook his head, saying:
"He does not wish the belief. The belief is a burden
His very flesh rejects. But we must believe, even though
It means we must lose him for a while and, in a sense,
Forever. He was not, as I always knew,
Meant to be this kind of shepherd." But Zipporah wept.
"It must be with our blessing," Jethro said. "We must all
Not merely bow but bless, we must will our loss,
For think what we stand to gain." And he repeated: "True.
The one. The great simplicity." But Zipporah wept.
And when Moses woke, bewildered, he sought his tent
Shivering, as though belief were an ague. Sleep now
Would not come, but a storm came, and he went to the tent flap
To secure it against rain. In lightning he saw Horeb
And cried in agony to it: "Who am I?
I am. No judge in Israel. Let the task be given.
To one of the wise. One of the strong. Do not
Place the burden on me. I refuse the burden."
Wife and son, awoke, heard, then they saw in terror
The naked body of the husband, father, hurled,
In another flash, as though taken and thrown,
And lie writhing, groaning, then still. The wife cried
Aloud to Horeb: "Whoever you are, what do you want of him?
Is it his life? For you shall not have his life."

Lightning showed metal, a blade. In the dark she groped,
Her fingers finding, as though told to find,
A shepherd's knife, his. Over thunder: "Take the child's
Life, if you must have a life," and raised it.
But with fresh lightning came the right words:
"Not a life. But a token of life. Not the body.
But flesh of the body that the body will not miss.
Will that satisfy you?" And, in an impulse, drew
Taut the child's foreskin and, with the sharp blade,
Cut. The child, maimed, screamed, clutched where blood
Flowed on to the flesh of his father, the loins of his father,
And the father stirred, groaning in air,
While blood dripped on the father. Then the father arose
And the child was in his arms, then in the mother's arms,
Kissed, soothed, while the storm traveled on
And dark hid Horeb. So morning came,
Fresh after rain, with birdsong, and the child was sleeping.
They lay in love awhile, and after, in sad calm,
Zipporah said: "Today?" Kissing her eyelids, he:
"It has to be today. It has to be. Alone." She wept,
He comforted, and they rose as the day warmed.
At least it was a known way. Staff in hand, he
Blessed, awkwardly, a family that had done with weeping:
"The blessing of the God of Abraham.
The God of Isaac. The God of Jacob. The God whom
Jethro has long sought. My love. My blessing.
The blessing of Moses. For what it is worth."
And then: "We shall be together. In the
Time of the setting free." He turned and strode
Uphill to the solitary palm, blessing that too,
Then engaged the desert. But he already knew the desert.
It was Moses he did not know.

4 | THE RETURN INTO EGYPT

AARON dreamed of an eagle made of fire,
Consuming, unconsumed, swooping out of the sun,
Yet this time not, as in the other dreams, in the desert,
But here, in Pithom. And as it swooped, men ran
To hide in their own long shadows. He awoke
To a relay of distant cockcrows. His wife Eliseba,
Eleazar his son, slept on. He lay, loving and troubled,
As the light advanced, dreading action, longing for action.
(Alive, at least they were alive, they could live out their lives.
No man could have everything.) Sighing, he arose,
And he took his dream to Miriam's house, but she
Had left her pallet, earlier than he, her children
Undisturbed, happy in sleep. At least the children
Knew no other life. Was it right then to impose
The promise of long agony on them? Troubled, he walked
Down the street of the workers' dwellings, open doors,
Bodies obscenely huddled, flies, ordure.
(Better the long agony, but still agony,
Still long, perhaps endless.) Where the slave town ended,
Miriam the widow cleaned out the bulrush cages
She had woven for doves, and the white doves throbbed around
      her.
Miriam the prophetess, as some called her, prophesying
The long agony, but then freedom, whatever that was,
Vigorous, laughing often, smiling now at her brother,
A question in her smile. "I saw him again,"
Aaron said, sighing. "This time as an eagle,

Flying almost above us here. No longer in the desert.
I know what it means. It means he is close to us.
It means I must go to meet him. I know, I know."
She said: "You still have too much doubt, like the others.
But for the others there is excuse. None remembers him.
Or, if he is remembered, it is in the wrong way—
A far-off hero who could tame snakes, who could
Strike men dead with a glance. Here once and hence,
They accept or half-accept, may come again.
But *again* is a future so far off as to be a
Sort of past. A past like the beginning of the world.
For us it is different. For our mother and father
It was different, though they had to die with the hope
Not yet bursting into dreams. Your dream is clear.
I have silver hidden in the house. We need to bribe,
Our overseer is bribable enough. You need to go
Over the river." He said: "Silver? Where from?"
And she, laughing: "Theft can be a virtue.
You seem shocked. There is too much virtue in you,
Virtue meaning timidity." Laughing, launching a dove
Into the light. He nodded, troubled, knowing it true:
Why was the long agony reserved for him
Who would have been content with quietness, or with words,
The action left to his son, or his son's son?
So, when the workday started, he trudged to the river,
The ferry just arriving, loaded with farmers,
A bull calf snorting at a flutter of squawking hens.
The boat emptied, the ferryman, black, from the south,
His carven face swimming with light, swigged from a jug,
Sour-faced on a mouthful of sour wine. Aaron said:
"Will you take me to the other side?"—"Double fare.
A lot come into Egypt. Not a lot
Go out, as you see. It's always double fare."
Aaron said: "But you have to go back there anyway—"
"Always double fare. Some are very glad
To be paying double fare." So it was double fare.
The ferryman was curious: why the journey? And then,
Incredulous: "A dream? You say a dream? You
Seek somebody because of a dream? Paying double fare too.

A dream?" Aaron said: "There was a time
When dreams were considered important in Egypt."
The boatman spat. "That was Joseph. The old days.
My grandfather told me about him. This is today.
All science today. Nobody follows dreams, not any more."
Aaron said: "I do. There was a time
When I did not. But I follow this dream. I have to."
The ferryman said "Then you're mad." Aaron spoke angrily:
"I see. And the rest of the world bursts with sanity,
Is that it? Mad because I dreamed of the coming of
Salvation? The others sane because they are slaves—
Is that it?" The boatman earnestly said (and would have
Laid a hand on Aaron's arm had not his hands
Been engaged in rowing: 'Never be taken in by
Words is what I say. Say that word slavery
And it sounds bad. Say instead a mouthful of bread
And fish and palm wine for a day's work and it sounds
A great deal better. Who is this one you're going to meet then?"
Aaron told him. "Hear that, you fish down there?
He's going to meet his brother and his brother
Is going to save the world. Look." (Earnestly,
Squinting at Aaron across the blinding river light.)
"If you're going to have salvation, as you call it,
It won't be through your brother or my brother or
Through anybody else's brother. Forget all about it.
You're wasting your time. Nobody's coming from over there.
This Lord God you talk about has forgotten.
He has other things on his mind. Let me take you back."
But Aaron smiled. "You seem," said the ferryman, "to be a
Decent sort of a man. Touched, a bit, but that may be the sun.
I'll take you back. I'll return your fare to you.
Half of it anyway." But Aaron smiled. The fight, he saw,
Was a fight against men who, ferrying from bank to bank,
Believed they were traveling. Good men, no doubt of it.
Given time, they could be fought with words. Words:
Words were a comfort as well as a weapon. So he landed,
Sketched a blessing, smiling, and the ferryman
Offered a swig of sour wine. Then, head shaking,
He waited for a boatload of the sane, seeking the world,

Egypt. Aaron now left the freedom of slavery
And sought the prison of the desert. Solitary, terrified,
When night fell, of the geometry of the stars,
He spoke to himself, or to someone: "There is, you see,
The question of convincing them. So set,
All of them, in their ways. Made soft by slavery.
Who is he? Who? Never heard of him. Show us a
Sign. Give us a sign. What signs does he have?
Does he have any signs? Signs are what we need. Signs.
You know what we mean? Signs. Signs. Signs.
Something out of nothing. Miracles,
Miracles is the word. You know the word. Miracles."
A star shot. The sky swung like a pendulum.
Then day, a mirage of green, mirage of a caravan,
Vultures gyrated, swooped. The corpse of a dog
In the rocks. Vultures swooped. "Listen, Moses.
Listen, brother. Brother. You know that word?
You know these words I speak now? The joys of
Slavery. The relief at not having to be
Free any more. A terrible word, freedom.
We are degraded, yes. But it is hardly our fault,
Is it, hardly our fault? Sodomy, bestiality,
Inhumanity. Hardly our fault. Only slaves.
We are only slaves. You see, Moses? Do you
Understand the words I speak to you, Moses?"
A black sky, starless, with a dying moon.
"Signs. You know, signs. You know what we mean?
Signs, signs." Day and a fierce wind and he lay then
Talking talking, half-buried in a sand drift,
Sand in the furrows of his face, till a hand came
Gently to clear the sand, and he saw the hand,
The arm. It was the eyes, he knew the eyes then,
And the mouth quiet in the beard of one who, he saw
With shock, was no longer young. Said to himself: No word.
And no word. It is the first sign. No word.
For though the word is in him it is I I I
Who must speak the word. And so, together,
With few words, words unneeded, they
Stumbled back into Egypt. And, in black night,

Unseen to Miriam's house in Pithom. Unseen
But heard of, guessed at. There was a morning
When the whip was hardly felt: *Came two days ago*
Over the river. And the children talked: "Gave signs.
Turned his stick to a snake."—"But signs of what?"
"Signs that he is a god. They're always saying
That we're going to have a god. Well, here he is—"
"But what is a god *for?*" And the old men talked:
"Something about his arm having leprosy on it.
Then he puts his arm in his robe and pulls it out
And the leprosy's gone."—"That's an Egyptian trick.
He sounds like an Egyptian to me. Somebody coming
To make us all work harder." But Dathan, plumper now,
His linen bright, his fingers flashing in the sun,
Spoke of the newcomer not to fellow slaves
But to the enslavers: "Moses. Brother of Aaron.
The one who killed the Egyptian and ran away.
He's back now, thinks no one remembers."
What is all this? What tale do you think you're . . .
"True. Look, sir, I was always a friend of Egypt.
I can give good information. Valuable. This Moses
Is up to no good. I would appreciate,
Sir, a little Egyptian generosity . . ."
To work. You are drunk. Go on, friend of Egypt.
Young girls spoke of a god, golden-haired,
With a firm strong body, young, bearing comfort,
Making life easier (said the older women).
But to Aaron fell the task of talk, to the elders,
To the young who bore authority: Joshua was one,
Hard-eyed but supple of thought, as though thought
        were muscle.
"What god?" an elder said, and, patiently,
Aaron: "The God who spoke from the burning bush
On Mount Horeb. The bush burned and was not consumed.
And the voice said: I am the God of Abraham,
Of Isaac, Jacob. I am mindful of the agony
Of my people. I am sending one who shall
Set my people free." But another elder, doubtful:
"It is the notion of the one god that I

Find tough to eat. What is this god's position
In relation to the other gods? That, I would say,
Is a reasonable thing to ask." Patiently, Aaron:
"There are no other gods. God is God.
The God of the Israelites is God, the one God—"
"The one remaining god, is that what you mean?"
"Our thinking," Aaron said firmly, "has become
Egyptian thinking. The Egyptians see the world
As multiple, various. Do you understand me?
There are, they say, many things in the world of sense
And, so the Egyptians argue, there must accordingly
Be many beings in the heavens, matching, ruling
The many things of earth. We Israelites
Never believed that. In the beginning we knew
That all was one, that All was made by One.
We forgot that knowledge. Now, my brothers, we are
To remember that knowledge. Remember it in action.
It is that knowledge that is to set us free."
And an elder wavered in doubt: "Free—you mean
Free to leave Egypt?" Aaron said: "Just that." And Joshua:
"Mere knowledge, I would say, sets no man free.
Man, I would say, does not find freedom through God,
But God through freedom." Aaron: "And how does he,
How do we find freedom? We cannot fight
These Egyptians with Egyptian weapons. We have no
Battering rams or crossbows. We can achieve freedom
Only by knowing the power of God and knowing
That one man can call down that power."—"Knowing?"
"You have heard of the signs. Of the miracles."—"Heard, yes.
But seen, no."—"You will see, will certainly see.
But meantime you must believe."—"*Must? Must* believe?"
"A man must believe there is a better life
Than this life of bondage. Our God is not a
God of slavery." An elder shook his head:
"If you say there is one God, then it is this
One God that has sold us into slavery." And another:
"Or else one could say that there are at least two Gods—
One to enslave and one to free. And to have two Gods

Is the beginning of having many gods. So we are back where
    we started."
Aaron cried: "No. Not that. Cannot you see
That our God may have let the wicked work on the innocent,
The enslavers enslave the enslaved? God will in no wise
Interfere if he sees not fit to do so.
Is this our bondage not perhaps a test,
A proving of our right to be the
Chosen of God?" An elder said: "Unconvincing.
I am unconvinced." Caleb, another of the young,
Spoke boldly: "There are weapons other than
Bows and battering rams and pitchballs.
There are bricks and mattocks. There are muscles—"
"Fools, fools," cried Aaron. "Egypt is the world.
Only the maker of the earth and sun and stars
Can prevail over Egypt. God is our way, God.
And our way to God is through him." Head-shakings.
"Him that is come." Wistfully one old man said:
"Free to leave Egypt. We are all, I fear,
Growing too old for that kind of freedom." But Joshua,
A trumpet to that plaintive piping, said: "We
Will help you to courage. None is too old to be free.
We, the young." Head-shakings still: "I am not convinced—"
"Nor I. Very far from convinced. Convinced. Nor I.
In the house of Aaron, at sunset, a ceremony,
A celebration: the bathing and clothing of Moses
For his visit to the Pharaoh. It was women's work,
And they sang, bringing water from the well, a song of water,
How water would yield to man, but only so far,
Water as flood or river or sea, never yield.
And Moses, smiling in a fodder trough turned to a bath,
Was laved by his sister, who said, clucking: "So dirty.
It seems you carry the dirt of a twelve-month journey."
And Moses: "Dirty or not. Yon know that. It was I."
Nodding, "I knew. I will always know. Remember your name:
It means I have brought him forth. And the I means I—"
"And yet you do not," he said. "know me. We have had
No youth together. Have not rejoiced. In each
Other's marriage. Or children. Though I can rejoice in

Your children now. If only I can find out
Which they are. Ah, I know. You are Lia—"
"No," said the child. "I am Rachel." Miriam said:
"There, *that* is Lia." And then: "My husband died
Soon after she was born. Soon after our mother . . ."
And Moses, sighing: "Yes. Before I had time. To know them.
Both dead. Too many dead. Before the promise."
Miriam, brisk to his sudden melancholy: "When do I meet
Your wife? Your son?" Moses, brightening: "They will be
Waiting for us. On the way. To the land. A long
Long journey. And we," in gloom again, "are not yet even
In the way of being able. To start on the journey.
My first. Door out of Egypt. Is a door into the
Very core and temple and shrine. Of Egypt. Pharaoh
Must be asked. Then begged. Then entreated. Then
Threatened. Then the threats. Mut start to be
Fulfilled." Miriam said softly: "It will be a hard time—"
"Ah," said Moses, brightening, "*you* are Elisa—"
"No," the child said, "I am Rachel. I
Told you I was Rachel." Moses begged graceful pardon,
Then said: "Hard? It will, I fear, be a hard time
For all the innocent. It is always the innocent who
Must suffer first. We sacrifice a lamb.
Not a crocodile. One of the great mysteries."
Then he turned to women's noises of pride, pleasure,
And saw what they had drawn forth from a hiding-place—
Cleaned but worn, ravagings of moth and white ant
But poorly disguised, that former princely robe,
Robe of a lord of Egypt. The smiles turned to pain
And puzzlement when he thundered "No" at them.
"No," he thundered, "I go as an Israelite.
I go. As what I am." And so he went
In the summer evening, in a pilgrim's jerkin,
His old rough cloak, carrying his staff, to the palace.
At first they tried to beat him away but he said:
"Moses. My name is Moses. Formerly a prince.
And still cousin of your king. I am expected."
So he was half-bowed in, in puzzlement, and was expected
In the room where the models of treasure cities,

Grain cities, were built. A new rich project gleamed
Among torches, candles, gold effigies, effigies,
Rich on the walls. Then Pharaoh entered, softly,
Alone, with the face Moses remembered, a clever face
Though hard (and it must learn, he sighed, to soften),
And Pharaoh said: "Is it you? Is it really you?"
Moses smiled. "I fear. I can give you. No
Proof of. Who I am." But Pharaoh: "The voice is enough.
Everything else is changed. But the voice, no.
That sudden cutting off between phrases, as if
Speech were sometimes being whipped out of you.
Moses. Cousin Moses. You look," smiling, "like a
Very poor relation, if I may say so." Moses said:
"You summoned me back to Egypt. I did not come.
Now I am come in my own time. But tell me why
You summoned me." Pharaoh said: "Simple. I could not
Forget you easily. Others I forgot—
Streams of courtiers, glorying in self-abasement,
Wise men, men who were called wise, sycophants,
Relations, none of them poor relations. A time came
When I felt homesick for you—you, the cousin
Who taught me, against his will, how to hunt gazelle.
The enigmatic prince of my boyhood. I must have been
A most unlikeable boy. I was, of course,
Too young to use you." Moses said: "And now
You are old enough."—"Old enough. Also," smiling,
"Master of the world, of the sacred blood of Horus,
Blood that, the poets write, is knitted from the stars.
Divine and holy, wholly divine, cousin Moses.
Gods work through men. And gods need men
Who know what godhead is. Do you still listen
To the voices of bats at nightfall?" Moses said:
"In the desert there are many voices. Voices
I had not. Heard in Egypt."—"You did not hear
My voice calling you? Or any voice
That spoke of me?" Moses said: "Yes. I did."
"A human voice?" said Pharaoh. And Moses: "No.
Not human. Not a. Human voice." Pharaoh fingered
An ornament, gold-chained, dangling from his neck, saying:

"Voices of the desert. That formless shifting world,
Whistling and singing nonsense. There is no
Solidity, no certainty in the desert.
Reality is here, cousin. For a thousand years
We Egyptians have been the masters of reality.
We have an exact and perfect, an exquisite,
An almost painful knowledge of the nature of
Power, power. The means of its acquisition,
Its growth, its maintenance. Power is here and forever.
This is the real world, and you belong to it.
You, who know reality, have been whoring too long
After dreams of the desert. You are recalled to
Reality." But Moses, softly: "Called, not
Recalled." And his eyes were lost an instant
Among the effigies, and Pharaoh did not
Well, for an instant, understand. But then he
Looked up, showing pleasure, for into the chamber
His queen came, and also a nurse, and in the nurse's arms . . .
"My son," cried Pharaoh in joy. "My firstborn.
Is he not beautiful?" Moses nodded sadly. "Beautiful."
Pharaoh took the child in his arms, saying in joy:
"My son. He will reign after me.
The unbroken and unbreakable chain of rule.
The strength which sets the desert winds
Howling in impotence. And you, and you
Choose these empty voices out of the dead sand.
This I cannot comprehend." Moses said:
"It is a simple matter, majesty. It is a
Matter of one's race. One's people. The
Destiny of that people. I have discovered
Where I belong." The child cried, putting out arms
Towards his mother, and Pharaoh kissed and
Hugged him, handing him reluctantly over,
The queen saying: "He is ready to sleep,
Now he has seen his father." And she left,
Looking curiously at Moses, whom she did not know.
"Where you belong?" said Pharaoh. "You belong to us.
To me. Bemused by the fable of your birth,
You ignore the truth. And the truth is that you are of Egypt.

Of the blood. For the blood is not what passes
From mother to son. That belongs to
The order of the beasts. It is rather what is of the soul,
Whatever the soul is. Your true physical mother
Was but the shadow. The woman who
Made herself your mother—she was the substance. She
Remains the substance, even in death. You, Moses,
You are of Egypt, and one of my tasks
Is to confirm that truth—in your own life,
In that bigger life called history." But Moses,
Impatient: "This is the. Mysticism. I must
War against. The voices of the. Desert spoke hard
Metal. The shifting. Swirling. Insubstantial.
Those are in your words. I reject Egypt.
I embrace my people." And Pharaoh, harder now,
Metal: "Your people, as you call them,
Belong to Egypt. They are the tough skin of the
Hands and feet of Egypt, no more, but the
Body does not disown them." And Moses, urgent:
"Beware of such. Images. The reality is that
We are a. Different animal. We scent our.
Own destiny. We must be free. To track it."
And Pharaoh, hard, metal: "Never. Never." Moses said:
"I know. You will never be. Persuaded by.
Entreaties. Egypt is locked against
Voices from the desert. It must be signs, signs."
"Signs from whom or what or where?" asked Pharaoh.—
"From the Maker of the World who is the
God of my people. The God. Of what he has made—"
"Signs?" cried Pharaoh. "Tricks? The Egyptian conjurers
Know them all. You are being the more Egyptian
For thinking of signs. What will you do, cousin Moses—
Turn that stick to a snake? My sorcerers
Can do that yawning. Make your snake swallow theirs?
We must from Moses, must we not, expect
Big magic? I should be appalled if Moses let mere
Magicians, salaried nameless men of trickery,
Beat him at that game." But Moses shook and shook his head.
"My Lord Pharaoh. Highness. Majesty. There must be

None of that manner of. Commerce between us. No
Ambiguity in your mind. You must believe that the
Signs and the demands. Come from a true. Israelite."
But Pharaoh could smile, saying: "You are an Egyptian.
Will always be an Egyptian." Moses did not smile.
"So you will believe. Until the signs
Persuade you otherwise. Let the tale begin now.
I shall not at first be in it. I am not qualified.
Being so. Slow of speech." And Pharaoh, smiling again:
"Another of your fallacies, cousin Moses."
But Moses was troubled at having to hate this man.

5 | THE PLAGUES

THUS, the tale beginning, the voice was Aaron's.
And all was done, in the beginning, to a
Strict pattern of decorum. For, to an official,
An overseer of overseers, Aaron brought the petition
That was partly a lie, but a lie was part of the pattern,
Saying, with proper humility: "Three days in the desert.
A small request, your honor. We have orders
To sacrifice to the God of our people." But the official
Stormed, according to the pattern: "Orders? Orders?
We give the orders. You interest me, little man.
Why in the desert?" Aaron duly replied:
"Since it was in the desert that my brother Moses
Heard the command."—"Whose command?"—"The command
Of Him who demands the sacrifice." The official said:
"You talk round and round, round and round—"
"Three days in the desert, your honor." The official said:
"Request refused."—"What request?" spoke a voice.
It was in the open air, near a half-built wall
Of the new half-built treasure city, and the voice
Was that of some peacock of the royal household,
Gorgeous, his face already an effigy,
On a horse sumptuously caparisoned. "My lord,"
Groveled the overseer of overseers, "this slave here
Asks on behalf of the other slaves permission to spend
Three days in the desert. Request refused, my lord—"
"Who put you up to this nonsense?" his lordship asked.
And Aaron: "With respect, we do not consider it

Nonsense. We must sacrifice in the desert.
You have your gods. We have our God. Only one.
We make no high pretensions." His lordship said:
"You have not answered my question." So Aaron answered:
"It was my brother Moses who in the desert
Heard the word of God."—"Why does your brother
Not make the request himself?" And Aaron said,
True to the pattern, "My brother is slow of speech—"
"And slow perhaps of understanding. When will you
Israelites realize what you are?" Decorously, Aaron:
"We are beginning to realize, sir."—"Take him back this answer.
And deliver it as slowly as you will." He raised his whip,
Its handle gorgeously patterned, and lashed. The blow was feeble,
Apt for the giver of the blow, but blood came
Rippling through Aaron's beard, first blood. Aaron bowed,
Humble, submissive to the pattern. But his word traveled
Quickly enough, Israelite insolence, to the palace,
And one day two high ministers sat at a game
Of senet, an intricate, geometrical game, one saying:
"Three days in the desert. How do we construe that?"
The other: "Israelite insolence, but we know its origin."
And the first: "Moses, yes. And what precisely
Is the present position of Moses?" The other shrugged,
Eyes on the gameboard: "The situation between him and the
Pharaoh—forgive me, I have that in the wrong order—
Is that he, of his own free will, has cast himself
Clean out of favor. I gather that the Pharaoh
Had an accession of chagrin, something to do with the past,
A kind of nostalgia, but that everything now
Is perfectly clear." The first one took a piece,
Grinning, and said: "The fable—you know the fable.
The lion prepared to eat the lamb and the lamb said:
Before I am eaten, sir, let me put my
Affairs in order. I assure, you, noble sir,
I will be back in time for dinner." The other laughed,
Examined the board, then said: "The Israelites, I gather,
Are buzzing with hope. There is a little device
I have always been interested in trying. Bricks. Bricks.
Have you had any experience of brickmaking? No,

Of course not. It is a simple process. Listen . . ."
So it happened, next day, at the mud pits,
That the workers stood around, puzzled, and the foreman,
Not Dathan, an honest man, sincerely puzzled,
Went to his overseer, noticing that, unusually,
There were soldiers around, and asked: "Sir. Where is
      the straw?"
There was no answer but grins began among the soldiers,
A kind of expectant lip-licking. "The straw, sir, straw.
To make bricks with. We have no straw. The straw hasn't come.
Straw." An officer said: "Do you have to have straw?"
The foreman, very puzzled, said: "What's going on?
With respect, I mean. Sir. Of course we have to have straw.
Mud, straw, water, the sun—that is how bricks are made.
Give us straw and we give you bricks. As always. Sir."
A scribe sitting by, busy with accounts, said: "Changes.
There have been some changes. Nobody brings you straw,
Not ever again. You gather your own straw.
Or you do without. Is that clear? Is that perfectly clear?"
The foreman frowned, very puzzled, and the laughs began
Among the soldiers. He took the word back to the workers,
And Joshua, one of the workers, said: "No straw.
No bricks. A simple enough equation." Caleb nudged him,
And Joshua saw soldiers with bows and arrows at the ready.
A deputation—Aaron, and Moses also,
But a silent Moses at this stage of the tale,
Joshua, Caleb, others, the foreman leading—
Went to say to what was now a
Grinning knot of officials, well-backed by arrows:
"Sir, sirs, with respect, we do not
Understand. If we get the straw ourselves
That doubles the work. I thought you needed bricks.
If this, of course, is just a way of saying
We don't work hard enough—I mean, you can have more bricks,
If that's what you mean. But give us the straw first."
The Egyptians said nothing still, but smiles were wider.
The Joshua cried out: "New Egyptian injustice!
We have had enough and more than enough!" The smiles went
And the soldiers were on to him. He spat

Lavishly into a military face, and then the fists started.
The other workers drew back—they had not meant this—
They had merely wanted to— Aaron looked at Moses
But Moses did, said nothing, abiding the pattern,
While Joshua was lashed to a whipping post and
Lashed to near-death. Joshua, when the sun set,
Still there, soldiers about him, guarding, covered with rod marks,
Dried blood, flies frantic around the
Wounds still open. The foreman spoke to Moses:
"You. You put the rod in their fists. You.
You'll put the sword in their hands tomorrow.
Or tonight perhaps. You and your brother.
This God of yours. I hope he strikes you down.
Both of you. Strikes you dead." Moses was silent
But the voice within him spoke bitterly to a fire on Horeb:
Why have you done this? Why do you bring only
Evil to your people? Why did you send me back here?
Why could I not be left alone? The sun dipped,
And soon the bats circled, whistling, and then the
Irrelevant constellations, no answer. No speech
At the table in Aaron's house—bread, fruit,
A meager supper—and eyes averted from Moses,
Moses eating nothing, Aaron little, his eyes
Not averted though very troubled. When Moses left
To look at the stars in bitterness, Aaron followed
And said at once: "I want no more of it."
Moses nodded. "You want to be free of me—"
"Free of this business," Aaron said. "Of having to
Speak in your name."—"You think it all a lie,
That the voice was a delusion, that I'm
Mad. Or misled."—"So our people think."
But Moses: "They think wrong. The voice spoke
True. It made no false promises. Nothing will be easy.
But the Lord did make. One error. The error of choosing
Me." They were both silent then and, for a whole day,
Silent with each other. Silent to his face the
People Moses was sent to deliver, but behind his back
Not silent. Children would throw feeble stones
And old men spit in his path, no more. Joshua,

Broken, groaning on his bed with the flies about him,
Was a sufficient witness against him. To the fire on Horeb
Moses spoke desperately: *See, Lord. See what you have done.*
Since the moment of my return there had been
Nothing but sullenness and a renewal of evil ways.
Your people are sunken into a deeper slavery.
You do not wish to set them free. He walked through Pithom,
So speaking, seeing whores offer themselves,
A young man sunk far in disease and neglected,
Children squabbling for a cheap Egyptian toy.
And are they not right to have lost hope?
Lord, why was it I who had to be chosen?
What shall I do? What shall I say to them?
And then the Lord spoke, but in the voice of Moses:
Moses. I begin now. Go to Pharaoh.
Say to him all that I bid you say. But the voice
Must be Aaron's still. He must stand in your place.
But you must stand in the place of the Lord your God.
So Moses stood entranced a moment on that street in Pithom,
Saying aloud: "The Lord my God." There were jeers
As at a madman. A stone was hurled, and not by a child.
But he stood transfixed, impervious. "Lord my God."
So there came the day, in a day or so, of the petitions.
A royal pavilion, with pennants, a throne, effigies,
Trumpeters, drummers, the whole court in attendance,
On a bank where the Nile narrowed, the water muddy,
Turbulent over a bed of slippery stones.
And on the opposed bank the suppliants,
With petitions for the Pharaoh, waited in the heat,
Swatting flies with palm fronds. Aaron and Moses
Waited with them. After hours of waiting,
Trumpets sounded, and a herald spoke:
"Whatsover person desires to present his
Petition to the most sacred majesty of the Pharaoh,
The divine Mernefta, must do so as follows. He must
Step into the sacred waters and be purified.
Thus purified, he may proceed to the royal shore."
Trumpets, then trumpets, drums, cymbals as
Pharaoh himself, well-attended, came to his throne.

On his throne, he saw many eyes quick to avert themselves
From blinding majesty, but the eyes of Moses
Were not averted. The suppliants entered the water
And, as was foreseen, stumbled, slithered,
Crawled back again, some, to their own bank,
While the court grinned, laughed when one old man
Had to be saved from drowning. Pharaoh smiled,
Perhaps dutifully, but he did not smile
When Moses and Aaron, upright among the slitherers,
Trod the riverbed towards him, Aaron crying:
"Pharaoh . . . we humbly request . . . that your majesty
Accede to our . . ." The king signed to the herald,
And the herald signed to the captain of trumpeters,
And the trumpeters blasted forth, so the words of Aaron,
Save for "strike" and "punish" and "revenge,"
Were smothered, and all speech and laughter smothered
When the drums and cymbals added their clamor. The eyes
                    of Moses,
The eyes of one who had foreseen all, held steady
And now Pharaoh avoided them. But those eyes turned,
Again as one who had foreseen, upstream where a
Man cried soundlessly, and the eyes of Pharaoh
Followed. The man was as though painted red,
And viscous red ran from him and he shouted.
Pharaoh stilled the clamor of silver and skin,
And the shout was heard: "Blood. The water has turned to
Blood." Laughter, and then not laughter,
For red was tumbling, sluggish at first, downstream,
Then bubbling over the stones, and the smell
Was, without doubt, the smell of blood. Moses and Aaron
Stood, as it surged about them, letting the others,
Terrified, crying *It's blood blood the water has
Turned to blood*, slither and stumble out, stood till
Pharaoh himself came down to the river verge and
Dipped his hand in. Blood. His eyes found the eyes of Moses,
And they said, surely: "Clever, cousin Moses.
But no more clever than my own
Magicians can do." And then they looked on blood.
Servants rushed with towels, wiping off the blood

From the royal hand, throwing the towels in
Blood, the towels filling with blood, floating sluggishly,
While the cry of *blood blood* went on, and Moses and Aaron
Strode through blood, their backs to Pharaoh,
Back to their bank. And now, all along Nile bank,
The cry or scream was *blood*, and in the fountains
Blood seethed and frothed, but in the wells of Pithom
Water sang clear. Then, from the waterways
Which were now boiling bloodtides, the frogs came croaking,
Blood on their skin, frogs countless, in droves,
With a deafening croaking, on to the land, advancing.
Water blood, and the land all frogs, then the air
Filling with gnats, beasts and men
Threshing and screaming, the sky black with gnats.
At the core of maddened Egypt, fires burning
To keep off the gnats, in a gauze tent
In a room of the palace, the chief magician used words,
Reasonable words, to calm the ministers, saying:
"Maintain, my lords, a scientific approach.
Approach by way of reality, by observation,
Analysis, never by way of theory. You ask:
Is it blood? If blood, whose blood? I reply:
That is not to the purpose. The substance, true,
Behaved like blood, smelt, tasted like it.
Whose blood? That is no question for the
Physical investigator. Think now. There are records
Of mud pollution of the Nile, followed inevitably
By an immediate exodus of creatures that live
And breed in clear water. Swarms of frogs and gnats—
Inevitable. We may expect also flies, locusts,
A murrain on the cattle—all stemming from
The pollution, by whatever cause, of the river.
You ask: is the blood, or whatever it is, a product
Of thaumaturgical conjuration? I say in reply:
The term has never been adequately defined. Miracle,
Magic—what do the words, scientifically considered,
Really mean? But, my lords, we have to remember
That this perverse and defecting Moses is, by upbringing,
Education, an Egyptian. He has had, doubtless, access

To obscure lore which, in this age of stability
And power, has never had to be invoked
Against enemies. To talk, as some are doing,
Of the magical potency of a new god, a god moreover
Of an enslaved people, is, to say the least,
Premature. Again, you ask: how is it that the
Israelites remain immune from these—nuisances?
The reason, my lords, may well be geographical.
Goshen, remember, is some way from the Nile,
Sheltered, removed from the causative pollution.
How dark it is getting." It was true.
They peered through their mesh at thickening air. Flies.
Thick, black, buzzing irritably, flies.
Clouds of flies. But none in Pithom. There
Aaron addressed the elders, saying: "The signs are before you.
Can you harbor further doubts? I know, I know
It is hard to take in. The God of the universe
Has chosen a people weak, enslaved, hopeless,
Indolent."—"Chosen for what?" said one. And Aaron:
"For the working out of his divine purpose on earth.
So it would seem. We must not ask too much.
What we must rather do is gird our loins,
Prepare for the coming of the day." But an elder said:
"The day, you mean, of leaving a bondage that has become—
Well, all that some of us have known. We are old.
It is hard to face the new life. It is a hard God,
This God of yours, ours." But Aaron cried:
"We must learn to think of ourselves as a people,
Not as mere tribes, families, lone beings with
Individual sufferings. Many of us
May be discarded on the way—worn-out, useless—
But the people goes on, the race continues. They that
End the journey may not be those that began it.
But we are all one, and the dead and the yet unborn
Share in the common purpose, the common goal."
And one said: "I don't like this sort of talk at all.
It's all blown up, like a sheep's stomach full of wind.
Life is, life is what we see, smell, feel—
The taste of a bit of bread, a mouthful of water,

Sitting at the door, watching the evening come on
With the circling of the bats. The things you talk of
Are only in the mind. We are too old, I tell you,
For this talk of common goals and purposes and journeys."
And Aaron was angry, shouting: "You speak thus,
When the Lord your God exerts himself beyond
What may be thought of as proper for a God.
For God has shown himself in the running blood of the
Rivers, in the swarming gnats and flies.
God leaves us unscathed and wholesome while all Egypt
Screams. Does this mean nothing?" And one said:
"It means, I suppose, that we are the chosen people.
Means we must face the desert and dream of the promise.
It means—oh, is it so blasphemous
To wish to be left alone?"

                              Then came the locusts,
Stripping the trees, save in the vale of Goshen,
Where Pithom sat. And then came boils and ulcers,
And lancings, and running of pus, the afflicted
Wretched, waiting in line for the lancet, and the
General wonder that things should be as they were.
Had the gods failed Pharaoh? How could they fail
One who was one of themselves? Was it some demon?
But no demon could be mightier than the gods'
Whole army. Pharaoh had done so much
To the glory of the gods—opulent monuments.
He had done for the gods far more than the
Gods might reasonably expect to be done. The pyramids.
Take the pyramids. To count the bricks in
One pyramid alone would take up years. What then
Had gone wrong? "They wonder," Aaron said,
In conclave in Pithom, "what has gone wrong. But they know
That we remain untouched, this they know. They fear us.
It is a new thing for the Israelites to be feared."
Miriam said: "We were always feared. If the Egyptians
Had merely destroyed us, our memory still
Would have been feared. There are many dead nations
That growl out of their ashes. But they brought us low,
They made us despised among nations. And the fear—

How is it now expressed? They are already beginning
To bribe us into leaving, to skulking out
In the dark." And she looked at Dathan, who,
In a corner of Aaron's house, gloated over
A little hoard of jewels and gold pieces,
Egyptian bribes. Dathan said: "I shall be happy
To take charge of all this side of our
Operation. We need such resources presumably.
Nor is there any need to wait to be given.
One may take. Take. There are any number
Of fine villas already abandoned. Death. The plague.
I knew some of the victims well. Through my position.
They're well served now, God curse them." Now Moses spoke,
Saying: "The potter has his craft, so has the builder,
So has the maker of songs. The Lord, too,
Has his craft. And it may be called. A
Dance of numbers. So far he has smitten
Egypt seven times. Rivers of blood.
Frogs. Gnats. Flies. A striking down of their
Sheep and cattle. The curse of the teeth of the
Locusts. Now the plague." On the mud floor
He marked in strokes with his staff to the number seven.
"The making of the world," he said, "was a dance of seven.
The bringing low of Egypt. Will be a
Dance of ten." They listened. "For in the heart of
Pharaoh there must be a kind of dance.
It must soften. It must harden. It must
Soften again. Must harden for one last time.
And then, like stone, it must crack. It must
Shatter. And Egypt. Must shatter with it. Delay.
Some of you think of delay. The young—Joshua,
Caleb—you think of delay and fret. But remember.
The Lord must have his craft. And we need the delay.
We must gather our possessions. Our carts. Cattle.
There is the matter of supplies. Grain. Water.
We must prepare. Our order of march. Think of the
Sick. The unwilling. The cries of those who
Would be left. To last out their days. In Goshen.
Women with child. Many problems. The question of

Unifying the clans. Creating degrees of leadership."
"The question of arms, defense," Joshua said,
Eager though battered, scarred, limping. "The army.
The training of an army."—"That too, Joshua—"
"The treasury," Dathan smiled.

                           In the imperial palace,
In full assembly, ministers about him, Pharaoh paced,
Hiding his deeper agitation, while a scribe
Read figures out: "One hundred and seventeen thousand
Five hundred and sixty-seven. That is the latest
Computation, your divine majesty." Pharaoh said:
"I am not greatly interested in numbers. So many dead,
So many lost cattle, devastated fields. It is not
Flesh and bone and possessions that we lose,
For these can be replaced a millionfold.
It is the heart of the empire, the central idea . . ."
And a minister said, in pain: "With respect, majesty,
You cannot so easily ignore the suffering of
Your subjects. It is an essential in kingship:
The king must see himself as a head, his kingdom the body.
Must not the head feel the anguish of the body?" But Pharaoh:
"It is the heart that feels, not the head.
The head must be clear. The heart clouds and confuses.
Let us hear no talk of feeling. Thinking—
That concerns us now." But the minister cried:
"If you had suffered—if you had lost—" And another:
"If I may say this, majesty, our friend is distraught.
He has lost both wife and daughter." But Pharaoh said:
"He can have another wife within a day.
Another daughter within a year. I do not wish
To listen to womanish laments and improper rebukes.
Let us quieten our hearts. Let the head speak. Listen."
And they listened. Pharaoh said: "This empire, Egypt,
Is the greatest the world has ever seen, perhaps
The greatest it will ever see. Our cities
Are crammed with all manner of merchandise, our ships
Sail all the known seas. Our towers kiss heaven,
Our armies shake the earth. We prosper, prospered . . .
At the very core of our empire lies a truth.

Or shall I say a belief that has long been taken
For a truth—the belief that the ruler of the empire
Has been appointed by the gods themselves,
That the Pharaoh is the issue of their flesh. How then can
The Nile fail to bless the land, the land
Fail to groan with the overwhelming
Blessing of increase? But now the gods
Seem to turn against their own flesh. Starvation.
Disease. Dissension. Fratricide. Distrust of authority.
Why? Why? Can the changeless gods then change?
Can the eternally strong grow weak? Can, from nowhere,
A new god appear to overthrow the
Tables of the eternal?" The chief magician spoke,
After a pause: "Your majesty has touched upon
An interesting, indeed compelling, theological point.
The gods are the gods, eternal, self-created,
Subsisting out of time. There are no new gods.
But, your majesty, the gods, so we must believe,
Have no essential interest in human affairs.
It is only by virtue of prayer, sacrifice,
The raising of monuments, even the skills of conjuration,
That they can be swirled into the human orbit.
Now, as it seems to me, one god forgotten,
One long removed from the concerns of the state of Egypt,
Has been conjured. You know which god. You know
By whom." A nerve beat on Pharaoh's brow.
Then he said: "You take us back to an old time—
A time when the false belief in a
Single god possessed many of the most subtle and
High-placed of Egyptians. You refer to Moses.
This belief has come back and it has attached itself
To a race of slaves." The chief magician said:
"Logical, majesty, as you will admit. Will the slaves
Willingly embrace the gods of their masters?
These questions, as I said, are of immense
Theoretical interest, but—there remains
The matter of what is to be done. I would, I know,
Be overtreading the bounds of my office if I
Ventured to—" But the first minister cut in with:

"It is a simple matter, divine majesty.
The devotees of the god ask that they may do
Sacrifice to him. They request three days
Away from their holy work of building monuments
To the glory of the true gods of imperial Egypt.
It would be a mark of kingly clemency to grant . . ."
And Pharaoh cried: "Be forced to grant, impelled to?
For the slave to cease to be a slave? For the
Power of his God to be recognized, acknowledged?"
"Only three days, majesty. With guarantees of return—"
And Pharaoh began to see what was meant. "Guarantees?"
He smiled. —"Guarantees, your divine majesty."
Then the hailstones came, thudding on the streets
And roofs and deafening, and, landing,
Spurting out flame. But not in Goshen, land of
Servitude but also of sun and clean water. From Pithom
Moses and Aaron came to the palace, knowing it was
Time to ask again, and were admitted to a
Dark chamber full of candlelight, where magicians
Consulted entrails, burned rare gums and powders,
Intoned in an old tongue. Pharaoh was there.
Aaron spoke at once, saying: "We are come again,
King of Egypt, to ask that we be released
From our labors in order to . . ." Pharaoh ignored him,
Addressing Moses instead: "Have you no respect
For our religion, cousin? We are at holy work.
We seek to avert these inexplicable nuisances
From the innocent Egyptian people." Aaron said:
"Not innocent. Not inexplicable." Pharaoh sighed,
Saying: "Our ceremonies are tainted by the presence
Of the unbeliever. Go." And the magicians
Put out their fires, made obeisance, departed.
"You seem to have reached the limit, clever cousin,
Of your resources," Pharaoh said. "This magic
Hail of yours can harm no one." Aaron replied:
"Harm was never intended. Not at first.
It was thought the signs of God's power would be enough."
But Pharaoh ignored him still, fixing Moses
With a look malevolent, admiring, even affectionate.

And Aaron: "Do we have an answer, sir? May we
Take an answer back to our people?" Pharaoh still
Ignored him, addressing Moses: "Are you pleased
With your power, cousin? Does it satisfy you
To have impaired, even part-destroyed, this great
Flower of order? Do you wish me to bow down
To a god who is the enemy of the State?
For, believe me, the State can be hated only by the
Eternal forces of disruption, a little of whose power
You have, through your trickery, shown us.
Without the State we are nothing, any of us.
Order, beauty, majesty, the unbroken
Chain of rule. To destroy the State
Is to betray us to those windy voices out there in the desert.
You wish to see Egypt become broken stone,
Lizards sunning themselves on broken stone."
Then Moses spoke: "You cannot. Maintain order—"
Pharaoh feigned amazement: "You have recovered your voice?"
"Cannot. Maintain order. On slavery." Pharaoh cried:
"What slavery? Any slavery? Or merely the
Slavery of your people? If you were to be made free,
Would you not have your highest and your lowest?
Would you not build your own pyramid?" Aaron said:
"Sir, we need your answer." And Pharaoh, in scorn:
"Quiet, little man. I am talking to your better."
Moses said: "We will build on the covenant.
On the bond. Freely embraced. The contract
Between man and man." Then Pharaoh bitterly:
"Your high talk in a land you have turned into a
Charnel. I cannot stand your smell much longer.
You had better go." Aaron, eagerly: "May we then
Have a scribe called in? May we have this written
And stamped with the royal seal?" Pharaoh spoke still
Only to Moses: "The word of the Pharaoh, Moses.
You may go to the desert and perform your sacrifice.
I have, may the gods forgive me, spoken."
Moses said: "You have not finished, majesty.
I would rather you said it now than shouted it
To our backs as we left your presence." Pharaoh cried:

"What have I not then said?" And then, quieter:
Ah, yes. The men may go to the desert
And do sacrifice to the god of destruction.
The women and children shall remain behind.
As this is a kind of war, cousin Moses,
Shall we call them a hostage?" Aaron was ready to
Rave, but Moses held him back, half-smiling:
"Your heart is still hard, Pharaoh. This must mean
You have not yet had enough signs.
Or enough suffering." So they left,
And Egypt, as Moses knew, was ready for the
Ninth curse. The hail had departed, the sun shone.
And God said to Moses: *Take up a handful*
Of the dust of the earth and hurl it into the sky.
He did so, and blackness fell. Thick, palpable
Dark in a black dark wind that doused all lights.
Nor did the other curses abate—the water blood,
Frogs, gnats, flies, locusts, murrain, plague,
Hailstones that flamed fire. Misery.
Deathcarts through the dark. So as foreseen,
Moses and his brother were summoned again to the palace,
But this time met by a minister, who said:
"The order is that you leave Egypt and go
Into the desert, there to conduct your
Sacrifice." But Aaron, quickly: "The women?
The children?"—"They are to go with you."
Moses waited, holding Aaron back,
Aaron anxious to leave, so the minister said:
"You expect something more?"—"Something more—"
"There is nothing more in the royal instructions."
"Nevertheless," said Moses, "there is something more.
We must wait for that something more." The minister cried:
"What manner of man are you? If you wish something more,
You may have it from me—the loathing of
One who did ill to no man and yet was compelled
To suffer. Who lost two of his dearest— No matter.
You are stone men. You ask something more
That our suffering may be prolonged. Go. You heard the order.
See—it is written clear. Why can you not go?"

And a voice said: "Yes. Why can they not go?" The Pharaoh
Stood by a door of ornate gold, attended
By torchbearers, cold loathing on his face, saying:
"They cannot go because they know there is something more.
What is the something more? You, Aaron, his voice—
What is it?" Aaron said: "We are to go
Into the desert for three days, there to do sacrifice
In the middle of the month of Nissan. Men, women, children.
With our beasts, our goods—" But Pharaoh cried out: "No.
You have eaten of the bread of Pharaoh, drunk his wine.
For three days you shall neither eat nor drink.
You will sacrifice fasting. Then you will return.
Your beasts will bleat and bellow a welcome home.
Your pitiful goods will lie snug, awaiting you.
This is the contract. That the god cease his torments.
That you go forth for three days, three days only."
But Moses said: "This, Pharaoh, will not do.
Your covenant with us was broken. Long ago.
There is no bond between us. When we leave this land
It shall be as free men. Taking with us our wives.
Taking our children. Sheep. Oxen. Goods—
Such as they are. Not the paring of a nail
Shall be left in Egypt. Not a hair or a scale
Of the skin of a beast." But Pharaoh cried:
"You go forth naked. Naked you return."
"No." And Moses was not now slow of speech.
"Your heart is still hard against the Lord and against the
Servants of the Lord. The land has suffered,
The king of the land must see the suffering brought home.
There is, Pharaoh, one last trial, the tenth,
And it will still not fall directly on your head.
You will live, whole and free, to see
The Israelites leave Egypt. But the trial to come
Will be the worst trial in the world. Do you now relent?"
But Pharaoh said: "The Pharaoh is not threatened."
And then his stone face became flesh, then the flesh writhed,
And the tongue ground out: "*If I see your face again* . . ."
But Moses bowed to the word, calm, saying:
"So be it. This is the last time, Pharaoh,

The last time you will ever see my face."
They left the presence, the palace, walking surely through
Howling darkness, until, on Goshen's border,
They walked through howling darkness like a wall
Into sun, clean air, and the song of fresh water.
Moses shuddered. The last thing coming. The last.
The tenth figure of the dance. But Pharaoh had willed it.
Men will even their own destruction. A heavy burden,
Free will, Moses sighed to himself, seeking fresh water,
No torment in the world greater than freedom.

6 | THE PASSOVER

MOSES, in sunlight, with the whirring of Miriam's doves
And the cry of children about him, sighed and spoke
Softly of the Angel of Death. "Who shall describe him?
Or her? Or it? Like a trained hound of the hunters
He has the scent in his nostrils. He follows the scent.
He will follow the scent of the firstborn." Miriam said:
"You were told this?" And Moses replied: "It is the
Last thing. The tenth figure of the dance.
Four days from now on the night of the
Fourteenth day of Nissan. The nose and the teeth of the
Angel of Death will dart straight
For the firstborn. Whether Egyptian or Israelite—
It will be no matter to him of the
Separating out of the nations. Even the
Firstborn whelp of a bitch's litter. The first
Hatchling of the hen. He will go for the scent."
And Miriam, in terror: "For ours? For our
Firstborn?" But Moses said: "Have no fear.
We have a secret. We will put him off the scent."
So Aaron that day addressed the people, saying:
"With your loins girded, sandals on your feet,
Staff in your hand, you shall be ready. So says the Lord.
For the time is with us. You shall eat the flesh of the lamb
Roasted, eat it in haste. And the bread you eat with it
Shall be unleavened, shall be a bread of haste,
With no time for the leavening. And you shall
Season your meat with bitter herbs, that the

Bitterness of the exile shall be in your mouths
At the very door of the exodus. Kill now and
Pray as you kill, for you kill in the name
Of the Lord's Passover." So the knives came down
On the necks of the lambs, and Pithom was
All blood and bleating for a space. Passover,
Some said, what is Passover? Moses explained
In his old halting way: "We call it Passover,
And shall call it Passover till the end of our race,
For tomorrow we pass over from death to life.
And this strange supper we take tonight
Is a ceremony. We shall have need of ceremonies.
To remind us who we are. What we are.
Till the end of our race. And the lamb we kill,
Each of our households, the lamb we eat
Is an offering to the Lord, who leads us
In our passing over from death to life." But of that other
Passing over he did not for the moment speak,
Learning fast the beneficent wiles of the leader.
So Aaron said: "On the lintels of your dwellings
And on the doorposts, you shall daub some of the
Lamb's blood, as a sign." As a sign of what?
So the bolder asked, and Aaron said: "As a sign
Of the primal sacrifice, wherein we kill,
And of the second sacrifice, wherein we eat,
Marking the place where 'we eat' " [beneficent wiles].
The daubing was done and inspected, and, on the fires,
The tender flesh seethed, while in the ovens
The hard heavy bread was baked. So at nightfall
All were ready to sit, girded, sandaled,
The children excited, and there was laughter,
Even song, for the time was coming. "The time is coming,"
They said, but not really believing
For this was a ceremony only of deliverance.
But in Aaron's house where all the blood of Amram
Sat, fingering the bitter herbs, "The time is coming,"
Moses said, and shuddered. "This is Passover,
And will be so till the end of our race, to mark
The hour of his passing over." Shuddering. "But it is a

Terrible thing, a terrible burden, and the
Burden is just beginning." He put his head in his hands,
But Miriam held his shoulders, saying: "Courage.
Courage." Then all suddenly listened.
But there was nothing to hear. "The silence," Aaron said,
"Strikes like a new noise." Then Moses heard.
"He is coming. God help them. He is coming. Now."
Then, from afar, a scream, and another,
And soon the sound of wailing. They sat silent,
The meat grown cold on the table, listening.
Then the noise of a nearing wind at the door,
And the door shaking, but then the shaking ceased,
And the wind passed over.
                          In the imperial palace
They heard the wailing without, even Pharaoh heard,
And his queen, in the innermost chamber, listening dumbly.
The infant prince slept in his cradle, placed in the heart
Of a magical pentacle, and the chief magician,
His assistants all about him, intoned, intoned:
"For the safety of the house and all within it.
May the first nameless, who guards the doors of the eyes,
Be doubly watchful. May the second nameless,
Who sits in the doorways of the ears, be this night aware
Of the rustling and breathing of the malign intruder.
May the third nameless, who lives suspended in the
Air of the nostrils, smell out the evil of him
Who approaches with the intent of evil . . ." A little cry
From the cradle, and the king froze, and the queen,
But they bent over and Pharaoh said: "He is dreaming.
It is a good dream—see, he smiles in his sleep.
My precious. See, he holds out his little arms."
And he lifted the child from his cradle and held him, crooning,
Like any father, then said: "No harm, no harm,
No harm shall come to him, for he is my precious."
A sudden scream from afar stopped the magician's chant
An instant, but he continued: "And the nameless one
Who sits in the cup of the navel . . ." Pharaoh said:
"Be quiet. What was that?" And a minister, soothing:
"A servant, majesty. The child of a servant."

Pharaoh whispered: "Nothing shall. Nothing.
Stand round us with your torches. Burn your incense.
Say your prayer. Say it." So the magician intoned:
"Gods of the seven worlds, hear, harken.
Let the word of your servent be sweet in the ear
Of the guardians of the living. Let no evil
Touch your servant this night, let the dark be
Beneficent, and the vapors of the night
Be like the balm of the morning. Let the souls
Of the evil dead lie in sleep, unenticed
By the smell of the smoke that puts out the light
Till the morning comes again, and the world is living
And the sun blesses and there is nothing more to fear."
Pharaoh looked down on his child, cradled in his arms,
Looked and looked and did not believe and looked
Incredulously toward his queen and all looked and
None was in any doubt as a bank of candles
Flickered as in the draft of a great wind,
And from Pharaoh went up the cry of an animal,
Filling the chamber, the palace, spilling into the night,
Spilling into one pair of ears in Pithom, those
That had listened to field mice chatter and bats at nightfall.
The palace took up the cry and gongs and drums
Turned it to a geometry of lamentation,
While, like a thing of wood or metal, the king
Carried the child blindly, the mother following,
Choked in pain the gongs muffled, till they stood
Before a god of metal and Pharaoh whispered:
"What do I do now? Beg you to comfort him
On his passage through the tunnels of the night?
Beseech you to remember that he is still
Of your divine flesh, and to restore him to the light
Where he is—needed? Or do I see you already
As very hollow, very weak, impotent, a sham?
Am I born too early or too late? Does heaven
Remake itself? Has the dominion passed over
To that single God who was neither sun nor moon
But the light of both? But in your eyes there is nothing.
Your head is the head of a bird."

The mother took the tiny body, weeping under the gongs,
And Pharaoh turned his back on the god, looking towards
Goshen, Moses, saying: "Did you hear my cry?
And the cries of the other fathers of Egypt, mothers
Of Egypt? Go, then, Take your women and your
Unscathed children. Take your cattle and sheep
And your wretched possessions. Leave my people in peace.
Go, serve your God in what manner you will.
And come no more into Egypt." And said again:
Rise up and go forth from among my people,
Both you and the people of Israel, and go,
Serve the Lord, as you have said.
Take your flocks and your herds and bless your freedom.
Be gone. And bless me also. Me also.

7 | THE EXODUS

BEFORE dawn, with a foredawn wind blowing,
With the blowing of ram's horns, answering
From tribe to tribe, under the moon and stars,
They got themselves ready, hardly able to believe it,
Many sad at leaving the evil known for the unknown good,
Especially as the hovels emptied of chattels,
The meager goods were roped to carts, and
Home, such as it was, dissolved with the
Fading of the stars. There were tears enough
As the cocks crew, answering from
Village to village. The cows were milked in haste
And, lowing, herded for the journey. A choral bleat
Of sheep drowned the horn and the cockcrow. Oxen
Were harnessed. While Aaron marshaled the tribal leaders
And then the leaders marshaled the tribes,
Moses walked among them all, cutting off thought,
For thought was mostly doubt of himself, seeing
The women with child, the children, the champing old
Lifted on to oxcarts. The stars were gone,
The east promised another day of fire,
The desert beckoned. Miriam released her doves
And her doves flew eastward, into the light
That was not yet cruel light. Dathan was a flame
About the cart whereon the treasury was loaded,
Gold, jewels, all Egyptian bribes. Then Moses spoke
To the God within him, saying: "Be with me, be
With me," raising his staff, setting his face

With smarting eyes to the east, and so it began,
The ragged exodus, with none to oppose them,
Through the delta land, through scrub, then to the desert,
Already, as the sun warmed, the lineaments
Of fatigue, despair, the promise of rebellion
Among some who, tasting that word *freedom,*
Were ready enough to spit it out of a dry mouth,
Longing sickly for the slave's day, the known evil.
So Pithom was empty. In the empty house of Aaron
A lone dog crunched the paschal bone. In the
Empty heart of Pharaoh bitterness
Found a house, then the house grew to a palace,
Then the massive portals of the palace heaved to opening,
After the funeral, one of many, the priests
Giving unctuous comfort, saying: "It will pass
As a bad dream passes. For the pestilence is gone,
The rivers flow silver not red, the air is
Filled with the song of brids not the buzz of gnats
And the fretful cry of locusts. The land, you will see,
Will be fruitful again, your loins, you will see,
Will be fruitful." But the bereaved wept.
"The evil," spoke the priests, "that visited our land
Was an emanation of an evil people.
But the Israelites are no longer with us: the gods
Gave us a sign to drive them out of our midst.
And lo they are gone . . ." At Pithom, in the empty mud pits,
A scribe drank palm wine with an overseer of workers,
His occupation, for the moment, gone. "Quiet," said the scribe.
"The silence is a sort of memory of their noise."
"Not quiet in the other mud pits," the overseer said.
"He should never have done it. Now all the slaves—
Greeks, Berbers, the rest—want to go to the desert,
To do sacrifice to what they call their gods.
Of course, it could all be a coincidence—
The plague, the flies, the locusts. But the
Blood was real, though. Red, thick,
As any in a slaughterhouse. All against nature.
It was as if nature went wrong for a time.
And these—" He gestured towards the huge absence.

"These took advantage. They didn't cause it, no.
They pretended to cause it. Cunning." The scribe said:
"This too is against nature. This not having slaves.
How does one build a city without slaves?
A civilization—do you know that word?—without slaves
Is totally against reason, meaning nature.
You have to have slaves." So they drank palm wine
To protect themselves from the evil emptiness.
In that other emptiness, nearly a day's march done,
The emptiness began to fill with the
First of the new signs: a dust cloud swirling
And many fearful and talking of being lost,
*We're lost already, and look at this evil dust
Enveloping us, I said we should never have left,
At least we were safe there.* The words of Moses
Relayed through leaders to tribe after tribe:
"You say we are lost. But we are not lost.
You see this cloud of dust. It is God's sign
That he is with us. See how the wind
Drives the cloud before us. God works through
Everything. Even a cloud of dust. God works
Through the smoke and rain. And dust of the desert.
God works through this pillar of cloud. See—
How it moves ahead of us. It bids us follow."
Follow, some said, *follow where?* The answer was ready
On the lips of the leaders: "The promised land.
Where else?" *We shan't see much of it.
Not with that dust in the way. And then there's night.
What do we follow at night?* "The Lord," said Moses,
"Will think of something." And, indeed, at nightfall
A blinding company of fireflies, was it fireflies?,
Flashed into view. *Fireflies? Glowworms?* "Let's follow,"
Moses said. A pillar of fire, moving ahead of them.
They followed, marveling some, some grumbling.
How did they know it was not Egyptian magic,
Leading them back to slavery? Ah, slavery, some said.
The word is worse than the thing. But they followed.
And, in the council chamber, the Lord Pharaoh
Followed his ministers' words distractedly,

His ears still filled with the sobbing of his queen
And his own sobbing. "The shock of the people, majesty,
Has been, naturally, profound. It is manifested,
So to speak, in a slow numbing
Illness of doubt. Such doubt has not
Previously been known." And "The whole concept of the
Monarchy is inevitably in jeopardy,
Since there seems, in the eyes of the commonalty,
To have been a withdrawal of divine power." And Pharaoh:
"What reports from the worksites, my lords?" They answered:
"Majesty, the recent riots have been contained.
There has been bloodshed—a little, not too much.
But there has been what is termed in this message here
A slackening of fiber, the sense of a
Silent but massive insolence in the face of the
Threat of . . ." And Pharaoh: "Yes yes yes, and of course
The great evil is already a great dream.
Except among the bereaved." So one said:
"Wounds heal, majesty. A truism, but true." Pharaoh answered:
"Anger does not heal. Hatred. But then of course
Comes doubt—doubt as to the validity
Of the whole ancient system. New modes of justice.
New gods. Can there be new gods?" The chief magician:
"The gods, as I have said, majesty, subsist
Outside time. Only in time is change possible.
There are no new gods. You may, majesty, take that
As an irrefutable fact." Then a minister:
"History, as our records show, is full of the
Inexplicable. The sudden famine, the muddying of the Nile,
Plagues, storms—Nature is wayward, self-willed.
But this has nothing at all to do with the gods."
Pharaoh said: "Vague theology, half-chewed theory.
What is to be done? What practical measures
Offer themselves? The shoring up of a whipped monarchy
With the gods yawning . . ." The chief magician said:
"With respect, your divine majesty, such cynicism
Is in itself a corroborative of the already increasing
Popular lack of confidence in the . . ." A minister
Spoke firmly: "The following narrative is no lie.

The Pharaoh, out of his divine benevolence,
Granted the request of the Israelite work force
That they be permitted to do sacrifice
To their god in the desert. The period of leave requested
Was three days." Pharaoh saw. "How many days
Have they now been out of Egypt? Five, is it not?"
Five, five. "So," Pharaoh pronounced.
"We bring them back. Nothing could be simpler."
Nothing simpler. Smiles, but he did not smile.
At the end of the fifth day in the desert, Aaron spoke,
Dissatisfied, to Moses, looking ahead,
Pharaoh and Pithom already far in the past:
"The mistake, I say, lies in the organization.
Old men, hereditary leaders of tribes and clans—
What true leadership can you expect from them?
They will be good enough at sitting in tents, cross-legged,
Giving judgments on marriage and property. But for a
Desert march . . ." Moses looked back at Pithom,
Into the sunset, faintly troubled at something
He must wait for time to define, and said: "I know.
But this is no time to reorganize." Aaron cried:
"We cannot survive if we do not. Already
Water discipline is bad. Food is stolen,
Selfishly hoarded. We need police, weapons,
A disciplinary court." Moses said: "The time is not yet.
We are not yet out of Egypt." Joshua spoke:
"We're a five days' march out of Pithom. As for Egypt,
It belongs to our past, a past to be wiped out.
We are already living in the future.
Perhaps Aaron is too old to feel the flame of the future.
We organize in a new way—from within.
Not the Egyptian way. He talks of police,
Of disciplinary courts. That won't be our way—"
"There is only one way," said Aaron, hotly. But Moses:
"Not yet. I say again not yet. Nor is the past
To be wiped out. If all others forget,
If even Egypt forgets, we have to remember.
He brought us out of Egypt. Write that in your hearts."
Then Miriam spoke: "Many of our women, I fear,

Still have their hearts in Egypt. All they remember
Is gossip around the fountain at nightfall,
The daily baking of bread. They whine for it—
The bread of Egypt." Joshua said: "Even the young,
A few of them, talked about going back. To the
Only life they know—whips and tyranny
As part of the order of nature. But I dealt with them."
Moses smiled, asked how. "Talked with them,
I and some of the other progressives." Moses said:
"A good word, *progressive*. Progress means
Going forward. No matter to what. Just forward.
Tomorrow we go forward to meet the water—"
"Water to cross?" asked Aaron. And Moses: "Hardly.
No boats, no bridges, no fording places.
We have to keep to the western shore, upstream."
Joshua said: "Still on Pharaoh's soil. Or sand.
I somehow still feel him breathing down my neck."
"Let us," smiled Moses, "now do what must be done—
Go round the encampments. See to the sick.
Soothe the querulous. Put our
Fractious children to bed." Smiling. They all smiled,
With the first faint lines forming on mouth and brow
Of loving exasperation.
     And Pharaoh said,
From his chariot, in his ornate armor, the lines forming
Of geometrical pursuit, the squadron leaders
Calling out names, said to his chief of staff:
"A minimum of violence, you understand.
We are not fighting a war. They are no army.
Threats, however, will be much in order. Hostages,
Especially high ones. As for Moses . . ." *Moses, sir?*
"No violence, no. He is to be brought back.
Stand trial. A public execution. Formal charge.
Formal arrest. The charge? All the charges in the world—
Blasphemy, disaffection, treason, murder.
Very much murder."
     In rocky terrain, at sunset,
Joshua sat alone, fashioning a bow. Arrows,
Already fashioned, lay neatly by him. Then he saw,

Out of the sun, a cloud of moving dust,
He peered narrowly, then ran to make his report.
But Moses already had heard, saying to Aaron:
"You hear nothing?"—"Nothing unusual." Moses said:
"Pharaoh must know I can hear him. We expected this."
Joshua running towards them, pointing. "A cloud of dust,"
Moses said. "The dust of his chariots. The masters
Are coming to reclaim their property." And Joshua:
"What do we do? What do we fight with? I always said
That sooner or later it would be a matter of fighting—"
"Sooner or later, yes," said Moses. "But not now.
We do not fight the Egyptians. Nor do we
Go back into slavery. What is left to us?
We progress, Joshua. We move on." Joshua, gulping:
"I say it with respect, but—" And Moses: "Yes, I am mad.
And our cause is mad. And the Lord God is mad."
But, those miles distant, at nightfall, Pharaoh was saying:
"They will never cease to be slaves. Slaves
To hunger and thirst, no doubt, at this very moment.
At least we can liberate them from that. Slaves
To geographical circumstance. They cannot progress.
They can, of course, go sideways like crabs. But,
Whatever they do, they are certainly pincered."
At first light, sir? "Oh yes," said the Lord Pharaoh.
"Their humiliation must be clearly visible."
But, those miles distant, at nightfall, Moses stood
On a rock, looking down into a swirl of waters.
A wind blew from the west. The voices in his head
Were louder than the turbulent Sea of Reeds.
Why could we not stay in Egypt? At least we were fed.
At least we slept in a bed. Egypt was home.
Some of us still want no other. Let us go back to
Slavery, as you call it. If that was slavery,
What name do we find for this? Are there not enough
Graves in Egypt? Dathan's words. Dathan,
Truculent with his rebels, crying out:
"Are there not enough graves in Egypt,
Since you bring us into the desert to find them here?
I was well enough off in Egypt. The lords of Egypt

Could be generous to those they knew were their friends.
Are there any ready to return with me to Egypt?"
And then the shame of it, Joshua's discovery:
Dathan and his runagates, stuffing into sacks
The Israelite treasury, then, discovered, crying:
"We were just protecting the treasury, no more.
There are thieves among us. I know what you are thinking.
But we had no such intention. We are all together in this.
We trust Moses. We trust Aaron. We trust you, Joshua."
Then Joshua and some more of the young progressives
Hit out, hit. Warm in his cloak, Moses
Reviewed all this sadly, snatching sleep,
Praying even in sleep, then waking to the
First streak of dawnlight, aware of
Some change that had dawned in his sleep.
The wind was blowing out of the dawn.
"The wind," he whispered, "is blowing out of the . . ."
And then: "Lord, if it be your will, if it be your will."
He stood praying as others came to see
The morning over the waters. They looked down in awe
At the waters ruffled by the wind out of the dawn,
A wind that seemed, oh God, to be parting the waters
As a comb parts hair. "Look," Aaron said.
"See what the wind is doing to the waters."
But they could not see what the wind was doing to the
Vanguard of Pharaoh's army, the pillar of the cloud
Swollen and all about the horsemen, the sand in their eyes,
And in their horses' eyes, hindering their advance,
Nor were their eyes turned to the west. Into the east,
As the sun rose, moved the Israelites, towards
Moses on the shore, making his decision, offering
A wordless prayer, stoutly raising his staff,
Then Moses, first, into the whistling wind,
Into the hair-parting of the Sea of Reeds,
Aaron after, the others after Aaron, timidly at first
But then with confidence growing—men, women,
Children, sheep, cattle, oxcarts, the young
Strong, fearless, the old amazed but finding strength,
And a child astounded at something in the heavens,

Unseen of the others, pointing, then hurried on,
The waters seething on either side of them,
But the channel near-dry and safe.
                                        At the water's edge
The cavalrymen of Egypt stood hesitant, seeing
Moses and Aaron on the farther shore, helping,
Bidding hurry, the eyes of Moses on the army
About which a dust storm whirled and howled, seeking
One pair of eyes for the last time. And there were the eyes
Of Pharaoh, seeing trickery, no more, evil magic,
Pharaoh calling: "Why the hesitation? Why the delay?
The way is open. Go for them." So the charioteers
Went hurtling into the channel, seeking that farther bank
Some of the old and feeble were slow in reaching
(A donkey grew stubborn, a cart wheel broke). But the wheels
Of the chariots did not break, rather mud and reeds
Clogged them. Then the wind changed.
The wind changed and the water tumbled in,
And Pharaoh did not think now of mere magic,
Seeing men swimming but trapped in mud and reeds,
The horses struggling, the chariots overturned,
Dumb cries in the tumult of water. The eyes of Pharaoh
And the eyes of Moses sought each other, but in vain . . .
So the crossing was accomplished. The Israelite camp
Was joyous that night with fires and wine,
The flute, the harp, the drum, and Miriam
Led the maidens in song and dance, singing:

>   The Lord is our captain,
>   His helmet the sun, the moon his shield.
>   The night sky is pierced by his arrows.
>   Halleluiah.
>   The hands of the Lord were with us.
>   They pushed the water aside and aside
>   Like the hands of the farmer dividing grain.
>   Halleluiah.
>   The horse and his rider were cast into the waters.
>   The Lord is just, quick to smite the tyrant.
>   Quick to heal the oppressed, comfort the afflicted.
>   He dips his sword in honey, in balm his spear.

Halleluiah.
We have seen the wonders of the Lord—in fire, hail,
Plague, famine, in the parting of the waters.
He leads us to a green abode, bursting like a pod
    with richness.
Praised be his name forever and ever.
Halleluiah halleluiah.

But there were some who listened to the tale of a child,
The child repeating and repeating to the questioners:
"It was heaven, I say. I saw it. God was there."
How do you know? Who has ever seen God?
"It was God, I say. A beast with a man's face.
And he was all made out of gold." *What kind of beast?*
"Like that one there with the cow, his mother."
"It's the children that see heaven," said someone drunk,
"That's well-known. That's written down in books—"
"I saw it, I tell you," said the child, "crossing the water."
Eat up your cake and go to bed. "I saw it."
Moses, grave amid the reveling, spoke to the elders:
"You must make it clear to the tribes. That the worst is to come.
It is good to rejoice now. If we are truly rejoicing
In the Lord. His goodness. His omnipotence."
And he looked with stern sadness on a
Passionate embrace in the shadows, the lurching
Of three men full of wine. "Tomorrow," he said,
"Will be a hard day. Especially for some." An elder spoke:
"The worst is to come, you say. It would be, surely,
Unwise to speak to the people of that. Is is not enough
To live for the day, hoping that the next day
Will bring sight of the land we are promised?
The day's march is enough, the repose at nightfall—"
"No," said Moses. "We enter on our inheritance
In the knowledge that freedom is a bitter gift.
It will bring many days of hardship. Shortage of
Water and of food. Sickness. Death. Cursing and grumbling.
Your task is to teach. The agonies of freedom."
Another elder said: "It is hard for a man to keep
Authority with such a slogan." But Moses, with energy,
With bitterness: "Must we build on false promises?

It is dangerous to think in terms of the day.
If we eat and drink what the day sends
We shall have nothing for the morrow. The day is for
Slaves. Slaves. There is a bigger time for men
Who are free. Let us begin by thinking of the
Week. The week." And with his staff he traced
Seven strokes in the earth. "The Lord took six days
To make the heavens and the earth. On the seventh day
He rested. We shall follow the Lord. The seventh day
Shall be called the Sabbath. On that day we shall rest.
Think of the Lord. Drink in new strength from the Lord.
And this this this shall be a law." *A law?* "And those who
Break that law must be punished." A third elder said:
"Punished? How punished?" Moses smiled a little,
Saying: "I will start to think of punishments later.
It is for the present enough to think of the
Lord's displeasure. There will come a day
When that will seem punishment enough. Punishment enough."
Dathan came with his friends to the assembly, drunk,
A bowl of palm wine in his hands, saying, slurring:
"Moses, we have come to express our
Complete confidence in your leadership." Moses said:
"You will always have confidence, Dathan, when things
        go well—"
"No, no," said Dathan. "Well or ill, we
Acknowledge you as our undoubted leader." And Moses,
Sternly: "I am not your leader, Dathan. The Lord God—
He is your leader. I am but his instrument.
Never forget the Lord." But Dathan said, tottering:
"Oh, this is a night for rejoicing, not for
Thinking about the Lord. We ask you, Moses,
In token of our amity and awareness of our confidence,
To drink wine with us." To which Moses replied:
"I have but a weak head, Dathan. But I am
Sincerely grateful for your confidence."
Then, with a drum thud, a flute skirl, and a
Sweep of the harp string, the evening came to an end.
You must make it clear to the tribes that the
Worst is to come. The worst. Starting tomorrow.

8 | MIRACLES IN THE DESERT

SAND-CAKED, sweat-blind, inexpressibly weary,
Through the scorching wilderness, Aaron panted:
"Do you know where we are?" And Moses, squinting about him,
Not showing weariness, upright, said: "The tribes
Called it the wilderness of Shur. We cross this wilderness
To reach Elim, Elim." And Aaron said: "What
Is at Elim?"—"Palms. Tamarinds. Water. It will be a
Hard climb." And Aaron: "Can they make the hard climb?
They need water in order to reach that water."
"They drink too much," said Moses. "The tribal elders
Are too old to set a good example there—"
"As I said," cried Aaron, "as I always said."
I'd give all his Promised Land to be
Coming home from work in Goshen. Water.
A bite to eat. More water. So they were all saying.
They came to rock, a rocky land, and Moses,
Showing no weariness, comforting the snarling weary,
Saw two young men, not of his tribe but of Joshua's tribe,
Wresting from a wailing group of the old a water skin,
Then drinking thirstily, spilling wantonly in the sand
Much water in their haste and greed. The old wailed.
And Moses said: "Theft, my brothers. Theft.
We will have no theft. They have prudently saved their water.
You have imprudently used up yours. Now you steal."
An insolent youth said: "Moses, this is the law.
The law that this desert of yours has taught us.
God made them weak. God makes us strong," water

Dripping from his insolent young mouth. And Moses said:
"The strength of the body is nothing. Is a crocodile
Better than a man? Men, my young brothers,
Are strong in a different way. What a man has
He has through foresight and prudence.
You shall not take from him what he has." And the other youth:
"What will you do to us, Moses?" Sneering. "Send down
Another plague? You would do far better to
Lead us to water. Including these weak and
Prudent snivelers here." And Moses said:
"I will lead you to water. In time. But now I tell you
That you must not steal." Grinning, "No more than that?"
"No more," said Moses, "for the moment. The time shall come
When we will try a man for stealing. Will exact
On the common behalf just punishment. But that time
Is not yet. For now, think that you are
Displeasing to the Lord. And that the Lord
Could strike you down if he wished. But that the Lord
Would prefer you to learn how to be men.
Not crocodiles." And he passed on. And they sneered.
But did not sneer at Joshua, the young, the muscled
Progressive. So the thirsty journey continued,
Until, in that rocky wilderness, under a copper sky,
The sun all burning bronze, they came upon
A spring, a feeble spring running through rock,
And they feebly cheered, limping with their
Pots and cups and water skins, while Joshua
And Caleb and the young of the tribe of Levi
Watched grimly, keeping guard, letting the old
To the stream first, trembling with relief and joy as they . . .
And then an old man screeched feebly: "No. No.
Nobody can drink this. Salt. It's salt." Groans
And spittings and the mutter of anger, then more than a mutter.
The sneering youth: "He said he'd lead us to water.
But what kind of water he didn't say." And Dathan:
"You said you knew this place like the back of your hand.
Every rock and spring you said you knew,
Every tree and stone. But you were lying.
Lying, weren't you? *The Lord* was lying too.

If he exists, that is. What now, great one,
Do you propose to do?" Moses, wearily,
Humbly even: "One cannot always. Be exactly sure.
We have been taken. So much off the path. That I knew.
Strayed sheep. Stragglers. I promise you, promise."
Faltering. But Dathan cried: "All promises.
Promised freedom, promised land, promised
Milk and honey, promised, promised. We can
Do without the milk and honey. We want water.
Water." That one word taken up—*water water*
Water water. And later, to the night sky,
Moses spoke, wretched, solitary: "Lord Lord,
What shall I do with these peevish children? Lord,
Tell me what I must do. Man is strangely made.
Fill him with bread, or water, and his spirit
Comes alive, ready to brood on heaven, on you, on
Human freedom. But let the meanest of your gifts
Elude him, and he croaks like a fractious frog.
Tell me, Lord, tell me. What shall I do?"
And what the Lord said or seemed to say,
Not from the silver and empurpled firmament
But from some dark small room in the skull of Moses,
Aaron, next day, would not at first believe.
Even in sunlight, the dead tree trunk in his arms,
Ready to hurl. "Throw," said Moses. "Believe."
And Aaron hurled the trunk into the salt stream,
Unbelieving. "Now," said Moses, "let them drink.
Let them at least taste it." Some tasted,
With sour faces of unbelief, then, believing, drank,
The wonder of thirst satisfied occluding
Simple wonder. Joshua, Caleb, others policed
The thirsty, screeching their joy, while Aaron said:
"How much longer will they have to be given miracles?
They cry like babies, expecting the breast
Always to be ready to be bared to them." But Moses:
"They must be led easily. Easily.
They have to be weaned into freedom." And the water
Bubbled in preternatural clarity and sweetness,
In potability, never-ending, and Dathan grinned,

Sleek with water, in forgiveness. "Weaned, weaned."
So the weeks passed, the days notched by Moses,
And the Sabbath observed, though not clearly understood,
With the cries of *water water* renewed, the journey
Upwards, over rocky land, the old and sick faltering,
The young learning to help the old and sick,
And Moses as weary as any, showing his age,
Till at last they reached a summit of rock and looked down,
And Joshua opened his mouth in joy and a cry:
"Elim?" They looked. Mountain beyond, but below
Springs, tamarind, palm, green grass like a
Torrent of emeralds. "This," said Aaron, "this
Is the true miracle." So they descended and encamped,
Some thinking that this was already the promised land,
The sheep and cattle going hungrily to grass,
The young bathing, playing in the springs,
The hungry eating dates from the date palms,
Sheltering under the palms. "The promised land?"
But Moses smiled and shook his head. At night,
Under the incredible heaven, the flute sounded,
The drum, the harp, there was song and dance,
And Moses, walking, came across love in the shadows,
A couple starting guiltily as the shadow
Of Moses came upon them, Moses saying,
Gently, always gently: "You, my brother,
I do not know. The woman I think I know. Sister,
Are you not the wife of Eliphaz?" She nodded,
Dumbly, and the man was ready to speak; truculent.
"Eliphaz," said Moses, "is old, near-blind.
He is content to play with his children, yours.
Youth is drawn to youth and to the
Lusty pleasures of the bed. I know, I know.
But it is a sinful bed." The man replied,
Truculent: "There is no sin in pleasure."
"Nor," said Moses, "should there be pleasure in sin.
For good or ill, a family should not be broken.
Your husband, sister, if he knew, could
Rightly put you away. And the children would grieve,
Lacking their mother. It is a bad business."

The woman spoke. "He knows nothing. We have been careful—"
"Not careful enough," said Moses, "to prevent my knowing.
If I know, others know. He will know. Soon, if not yet.
We face the hard task of building a nation.
The bricks of that edifice are the families.
If the families crack the whole structure totters."
The man said: "We are a very small crack. In a
Very small brick." But Moses: "Never think of yourself
As an exception that makes no difference to the whole.
For why should not everyone, if he so desires,
Be an exception? Only God is above the law.
But God works through the law. You, my children,
Are breaking the law." The woman said: "What will you do?"
And Moses: "I have done all that I wish to do.
For the moment. But remember—in your bed
Another lies, a third. He parted the waters.
He killed the masters who enslaved you. And already
You destroy what he bids you build." And so he left them.
The woman said to the man: "Does he have a wife?"
"He's old," said the man. "He's beyond passion. Love."
And so they fell once more to their embrace,
But she started, uneasy, thinking she heard
One of the children crying, and though he tried
To imprison her once more in his embrace,
She resisted, rose and left him. In an embrace
Wholly sanctified, Aaron and Eliseba,
She of the smooth brow and sweet tongue, lay,
Quiet after love, the children sleeping,
Fruit in a bowl, water in a pitcher nearby,
And Eliseba said: "Why then not here? Here
Is everything." But Aaron said: "Because the promise
Is to be fulfilled elsewhere, not here. Simple,
Simple as that." But she: "Will you live to see it?"
"If by *we*," said Aaron, "you mean our people—
Yes, I believe so. If by *we* you mean yourself,
Myself—I am not sure. But I believe our children
Will see it." She said: "We could settle here
Very comfortably. Fine pastures. Much water.
The whole place laughs and rings with water." He:

"No. We have to have more than a mere oasis.
We have to build a city, build a temple."—"Have to?"
"Have to, yes. Call it the fate of a nation."
She mocked gently, smiling: "Those big words."
Aaron said: "I do not, I think, believe
There is anything after this life. We die alone
And go alone into the dark. Us—you, me,
Each and all of the others. But all of us
Made into a nation—that is different. Here is a
Man called Aaron and a woman called Eliseba.
There is a new kind of human being we call Israel—"
"And where," she asked, "is this new kind of human being?"
"Trudging through the desert," Aaron answered,
"Seeking the appointed place. And still being made.
It is a formless lump so far—it has to be molded,
Kneaded, like bread. But when it is made,
This new being, when it lives and breathes and follows
The laws that sustain it, there will be no end to it."
She thought and said: "There have been others, nations.
They died. You told me once that Egypt is dying."
Aaron said: "We are different. We cannot die,
Because, for the first time, the nation will not be
Greater than the smallest within it. It will live forever
While men and women will die, but it will not live
By eating the flesh of those within it. Not like Egypt.
Do you understand?" She grimaced, saying: "No.
We had better sleep. Did he tell you all this?"
"Some of it," Aaron said. "Some of it
I worked out for myself." She said: "Poor Moses.
Alone. No wife. No children. Does he even know
If they are still alive?" Aaron said: "He does not doubt it.
Nor do I doubt it. They will be there, waiting,
Under Mount Horeb. That," he smiled, "is one reason
Why we hurry. Why we leave early tomorrow."
But so many left with regret, some weeping,
Some loud in anger at once more engaging the desert,
When here were date palms and springs and rest and pasture.
Soon hunger and thirst, under that metal sky,
Sand and sand and sand beneath, raised voices:

Good fish and meat and bread, onions, garlic,
In Egypt, Egypt. Why did you take us from Egypt?
We were happy there. And some spoke of the oasis
As a home they were wrenched from, till Moses rose and cried:
"Will you never cease to complain? Why God chose you
From all the peoples of the earth I do not know,
Will never understand. Did you not have your chance
To fill your store bags in the oasis of Elim?
You were careless, wasteful, improvident. Ill-disciplined,
Selfish, totally ungrateful. You say you lack bread.
You say you lack meat. Well, believe me—
You shall have flesh to eat this evening and
In the morning bread to the full. You have the
Lord's promise, through me, that this will be so.
And now you will smile, changing the set of the face
Like a child that howls to be picked up and then sees
Its mother come running. Ah, I am sick of you,"
Seeing the petulant, scolded children's faces,
Adding: "But, God help me, you are all I have."
But there was no petulance, only relief and wonder
When, at nightfall, a monstrous cloud of quails
Was thrown out of the sky. Joshua, Caleb,
The provident young, schooled by foreknowing Moses,
Were ready with the nets they had improvised,
And they caught the quails, and the quails were spitted
And roasted and eaten—another miracle,
And they were ready, picking the bones, to grow
          used to miracles.
Miriam said to Moses: "You take credit for
A miracle where there is none. You told me
About the migration of quails when we were in Pithom
And I was scrubbing the dirt off you." Moses smiled.
"I never take credit for miracles. Yes, the quails.
They rest at night in the scrublands. They are easily caught.
A miracle, I suppose, is the thing we need.
Happening when we need it. I suppose now
They would like bread to sop up the drippings—"
"Will they get their bread?" she asked, and Moses said:
"I said *in the morning*. I did not say which morning.

Have you heard of manna?"—"Bread," she said, "from heaven—"
"True, it comes from heaven, even when it is the
Resin that falls from the tamarisk tree. I have tasted it.
It is blown by a strong wind, lying like a gift on the ground.
A fine flakelike thing, fine as hoarfrost,
White as coriander seed, and the taste of it
Is the taste of wafers made with honey." She smiled.
"A poem?"—"A song," he said, "sung by Jethro.
He taught me the song and I sang it to Zipporah.
I sang it about the body of Zipporah—"
"How soon," she asked, "shall I meet her? And see Gershom?"
"Oh," he answered, "there will be more days of grumbling
And days of short-lasting joy. And, God help us,
There will be a time of bloodshed." He brooded, but she
Asked no question. He, brooding, looking into the fire,
Saw enough blood in it. But one thing at a time,
For soon the tamarisk resin came blowing in, another miracle,
So many miracles, bread from heaven: they crammed
              their mouths
Their baskets. There seemed no end to it, soon
No urgency in the gathering: it was always there.
But one day a family was manna-gathering blithely
And Caleb came to them, stern, to say: "Come.
You must come with me. And bring your baskets."
"What is this? said the father. "Why? Who are you?"
"My name is Caleb, not that it matters. You,
Do you know the law of the Sabbath?"—"What law?
              What Sabbath?"
The elders, sitting in judgment, were patient enough.
"The law," said the presiding magistrate,
"Has been clearly laid down. The Sabbath is for rest,
For thinking of the Lord's justice and goodness.
No journeying—so it is enjoined. No work." But the father,
Spluttering, indignant, said: "But we were hungry.
We were not working. We were gathering food—"
"You must have your food ready on the eve of the Sabbath.
We make no distinction between kinds of work.
Shear the sheep, mend a tent, gather food—
It is all work, and it all fills time that should be filled

With the contemplation of the Lord. Work must not defile
The Sabbath of the Lord."—"Mad, it's madness!"
"Oh, can you not see," the chief elder said, "can you not—"
But Aaron, silently arriving, completed the sentence
And added more: "Can you not see, you fool,
That if God rested from his work on the seventh day
Then man, made in God's image, must rest too?
That only to slaves is every day the same—
Toil, toil and again toil? That man, God's image,
Is not just toiling flesh but contemplative mind,
And for contemplation there must be leisure?
That leisure must not come capriciously,
Irregular, but in a known rhythm?
That leisure must be total?" And the elder added:
"Thus saith the Lord. Have *you*, friend,
Anything now to say?" And the man mumbled that he was
Sorry. "This is a first offense? Very well, then:
Discharged with a solemn warning. And, ah yes—
Go hungry till tomorrow." The father, mother,
Children looked glum at that. But Aaron smiled,
Saying: "Tomorrow begins at sunset today."
So they smiled and got them gone. The rule was mild
In those early days of the journey, the children of Israel
Truly children in the knowledge of the blessing of freedom,
The harshness of freedom. The blessing would be long delayed
In the eyes of the many, but the harshness they had known
Was nothing to what was to come: it was coming.

9 | THE MOUNTAIN

THEY struggled through the wilderness of Rephidim,
Where there was no bounty of quails or manna,
And soon, with their bags and water flasks long empty
They yet found strength to stone Moses, stone him,
For there was no shortage of rock. Aaron, Joshua, Caleb,
Even Miriam were swift to protect him,
The whole tribe of Levi, stronger-hearted than the rest,
Was a jagged fortress about him, but even there
Despair rose and the old cry of *water water*.
He could only raise his face to the burning sky
And cry: "What shall I do with this people?
Tell me, what shall I do?" The answering voice,
His own voice, was angry and strident, saying:
"Stride forth to the rocks. Strike the rocks
With your rod. They shall have their fill of water,
My thirsty people." So he struck and struck,
Rock after rock after rock, and it gushed out,
Silver water, and bellies and vessels were filled with it.
There was little gratitude: miracles were their due.
And Dathan was even ready to doubt the miracle,
Saying to his cronies: "See. Anyone can do it."
He smote a rock with his cudgel, saying: "See."
And water trickled forth. "Porous, you see.
This rock holds rain like a sponge. You hit it,
No more. The Lord God, indeed.
Cunning, cleverness. Anyone could have thought of it."
So they went about, hitting out trickles. The Lord, indeed.

It seemed certain to many that the Lord was not with them.
Never more so than when, one night among rocks,
The night fires burning out, on the verge of the encampment
Rods struck, knives struck, rocks rained,
And where there had been night quiet was shrieking,
Cursing, bellowing, bleating, and the
Laugh of triumph in a strange tongue. A raid,
With the carrying off of cattle and women,
Men lying brained in the sick dawn. Moses saw
And said: "The Amalekites. This is their territory."
Joshua cursed: "We are weak. We have no weapons,
None except these wretched arrows and bows.
I always said we should be ready for this."
A tremulous elder kept saying: "It is the Sabbath.
By my computation it is the Sabbath.
We need a ruling. Do we fight on the Sabbath?"
And Moses: "Oh, yes. We fight on the Sabbath."
Aaron looked on the crude weapons
Joshua had made, Joshua and some of the others,
And said: "When did you make these?" Joshua answered:
"In my leisure hours, such as they are, and, of course,
        on the Sabbath.
There was nothing else to do except contemplate God,
And this, surely, does not count as work?" There was silence,
A rather embarrassed silence. A young man named Koreh
Broke it by saying: "I have no experience of war,
Nor have any of us. Slaves are not warriors.
But I think I could suggest a simple strategy."
Moses said: "We are listening." So they listened.
When the next night raid came they were ready with
Lambs laid out as decoys, temptingly bleating,
And, when the Amalekites appeared, Joshua and his
Warriors rushed out of the rocks with rocks and arrows
And killed and put to flight, killing with daggers
Dropped by the put to flight. "Next time," Koreh said,
"It will not be a little matter of a night raid."
Nor was it. When, in strengthening light,
The Israelites, with goods and flocks and cattle,
Were ready at the mountain foot for the march,

Hidden among boulders on a high slope Moses stood,
With Aaron and Koreh, watching. He watched and saw,
In dust, the entire tribe of the Amalekites
Approaching in the distance. He raised his staff.
Joshua and his warriors, on a lower slope,
Hidden among rocks, armed with rocks, saw the sign.
The raiders came nearer, bold, seeing only
Tired wanderers and cattle and flocks,
And greed quickened their pace towards the prey.
So Joshua signaled and shocked them with a quick fire
Of arrows, till all the arrows were spent.
Then came the hurling of stones, stone after stone
After stone, for there was no shortage of rock.
They had not expected this, the Amalekites:
Howling, they turned tail, in spite of the
Howls of the leaders, their retreat thickening and growing.
And now was the turn of the hidden reserve,
Lurking behind the noncombatant Israelites,
Rushing on the rear, busy with rocks and daggers,
Picking up daggers. Carnage, delectable spoils
Of swords and spears, breastplates even, helmets,
For the Amalekites were a warlike people.
So as the Israelites trudged on their way,
There was a breastplate on Joshua, and a helmet,
And a dagger in a sheath—the general Joshua,
Close to Moses, and Aaron some way behind,
The office of Aaron somewhat less clear than it had been.
They trudged towards Midian, and the heart of Moses
Beat painfully as he said to himself: "Thick and strong
It beats, the desert blood. In the women,
As much as in the men. What law prevents her
Yielding to some young red mouth of Midian,
Black-bearded, a storm in the pulse? And, if she has waited,
Believing me still to be among the living,
There begins the double burden—that of a man
With two families, two." There it was, then,
At last, old territory, loved, fateful—
The solitary tree on the hill, the sacred mountain,
The wells of Midian and, yes, a group waiting,

Waving. Moses ceased to be a leader,
Breaking with an unwonted speed from the van of the progress,
Becoming the husband and father. Joshua smiled,
The Israelites waited in wonder. And so—Zipporah,
Gershom grown, Jethro old, the sisters
(Some married, one dead), embraces, tears,
And embraces and tears in the tent of Zipporah
In the following dawn, Moses saying: "My love,
It will take time for me. To be again what I was."
And she: "You have grown thin. You have lacked
Too long the roasted firstlings and the broth
Of herbs and mutton I cooked for you. Also the love.
You are very thin."—"Also old? Also very old?"
"I did not," she smiled, "say that. But you need time
And rest to make those eyes lose their fierceness,
Those hard lines round your lips melt to tenderness."
So they embraced, but a voice outside called: "Moses!"
And Moses wearily smiled: "So it will always be.
Israel lying in bed between us." He donned his robe
And left the tent to hear news of fighting.
"Reuben and Judah?" he said. "Impossible."
"All too possible," Joshua said. "Tribal war.
It was some matter of a woman." Bitterly, Moses:
"A woman. A woman of Reuben and a man of Judah.
Is that the story?" Joshua said: "A man of Reuben,
Single, and a married woman of Judah—"
"So," said Moses, "they've developed a taste for war—"
"We shall all," said Joshua, "need to develop that taste."
"But," Moses cried, "this is not a matter
Of repelling invaders. It is brother against brother.
Do not the fools yet see that we must be one,
One, one, not a loose parcel of tribes?"
Joshua said: "To be truthful, the possession of weapons
Drove them to the use of weapons."—"It is always so,"
Sighed Moses. "You must construct an armory.
You must keep our weapons clean and locked away.
If we are to fight with nations—then, so be it.
But we are not to make war among ourselves.
How many are dead?"—"Only one dead," said Joshua.

"A very small war. Caleb and I soon stopped it—"
"Brother killed brother," sighed Moses. "Cain and Abel
Back to life, or death. And was the man . . . ?"
"The man," Joshua said, "was the single
Man of Reuben, no longer able to love the
Married woman of Judah." So they walked through the camp
And saw the adulterer, pitifully broken and rent,
Lying on the ground, and the assembly fearful
As Moses spoke: "This is not war but murder.
The law says that you shall not kill, but we
Make an exception to the law. For if the enemy
Seeks to kill you, then you may justly,
And out of the need of nature, kill him first,
If you can. But what is your enemy?
He is someone remote, of strange tongue, of evil intention.
You will meet many such enemies, believe me,
Before you cross to the land of the Lord's promise,
And even thereafter there will be enemies enough.
But we are one, of common custom and speech,
And—note this, note it well—chosen together,
As one people, as one family, for the special favor
And the special chastening of the Lord our God.
Therefore I say this to you: that the deed
That was done was no brave deed of warfare
But a foul act of murder. And if there was a murder,
There must of necessity be one accused of murder.
Let him come forward." There was silence for a space,
And eyes turned to the ground, and the eyes of Moses
Saw that dead man as he had once been, alive,
Embracing lustily, and remembered his own words,
Gentle, warning, in vain. Sly, shamed eyes
Fixed on one young man, who now came boldly,
And Moses said, gently enough: "What have you to say?"
"I acted under orders," the youth said.
"We were ordered to attack the enemy."
Moses said: "There was no enemy.
A man killed a man and that is murder.
And what is the punishment for murder?
Let us hear from the heads of the tribes concerned."

These came forward, doubtful, and Moses asked again:
"What is the punishment for murder?" The head of Judah
Said, full of the old way: "The washing out of
Blood by compensation. Let the young man
Or his parents make good the loss of
An able-bodied member of our tribe.
Let us then have a warrior or a slave.
Or cattle. Or sheep. We can discuss the details now."
But Moses cried: "No! No! We cannot and must not
Value human life in terms of possessions.
For human life is precious and irreplaceable
And cannot be treated as a kind of money. So I say again:
What is the punishment for murder?" The leader of Reuben
Said, cunningly as he considered: "If we cannot
Put a value on human life, then we cannot
Compute the punishment." And Moses answered: "That is
Right. And yet also wrong. For human life
Can be valued only in its own terms. So I say:
A life for a life. Which means: a death for a death."
The silence was full of fear, and Joshua spoke
To break the silence, resolve the fear: "How shall the
Murderer—What I mean to say is: how
Is it to be done?" Moses answered, sighing:
"Joshua, Joshua, to think of that now. Did you suppose
I intended his immediate execution?
For *his* life is still a precious life.
The judges of his guilt must, as I see it,
Learn to revel in their own confusion, thinking:
Did he do it or did he not? Can the witnesses
Be trusted? Did not perhaps the dead man
Drop dead in fright when he saw the knife approaching?"
And he looked on the butchered body and trembled, saying:
"You have hardly begun to conceive, any of you,
Of the preciousness of a human life." Of this he spoke
To Jethro, in the pasture below Horeb,
Soothed by the old shepherd's trade, and Jethro said:
"Give them the law, then delegate, delegate.
Change now, now. This will not do,
This wearing out of one poor brain and body

In the service of so many. Organize, delegate.
And, first, get rid of your hereditary chiefs.
Heredity is not enough, it does not of necessity
Qualify a man to rule. Then remember this:
The basis of good government is the ten,
The ten, the ten. Good junior officers—
Each one in charge of ten. Then senior officers,
Each one in charge of fifty. Then you climb
The ladder—very good men charged with a hundred.
And then at last the cream—the superb, the
Incorruptible leaders of a thousand.
God-fearing men, trustworthy, humorous,
Preferably young men. There is no great virtue in age—"
"Men like Joshua, you mean," Moses said.
"He is one who carries the new fire.
But first I must tend his fire for him. Also,
Warm my own hands by it."—"Joshua?"
Jethro said. "Is he married?" Moses said not,
And Jethro sighed with a faint hope. "All this,"
Moses said, "will strike them as—subversive—"
"Good," said Jethro, "good."—"Somewhat like the
Organization of an army." And Jethro: "So it is. You
Are an army. But an army of human souls:
Let none forget that. You will be fighting
Your way towards this land of milk and honey.
The zest is all in the fighting. It will be a long time
Before the cows and goats are born that will yield that milk,
And for that honey—the bees must gather. A bland diet,
Very bland." And then the mountain shook,
As out of sleep, and Moses said: "It sounds
As if I am to be summoned. Ah, God help me."
Jethro smiled. "That, my son, is a prayer
You will be able to deliver in person." And Moses smiled,
And looked towards the rumbling of the mountain.
That day, with pain, he climbed it, saw that bush
That had once burned, but this time heard the voice
Come from the very peak, saying: "Say this
To the house of Jacob, this to the people of Israel.
Say: If if if you will obey my voice

And keep my covenant, you shall be to me a
Kingdom of priests and a nation of holiness.
But the choice is theirs, the choice, I say, is theirs.
And if they choose this covenant with me,
Then let them spend two days in the holy rites
Of purifying themselves. On the third day
I will come in a thick cloud on the mountain top.
What I speak with you the people shall hear,
And may also believe you forever. And the words
        of the covenant
Shall be set down on stone imperishable,
That they may be beheld by the eyes of men."
The peak was silent, and so Moses descended
To the world of his waiting people, bidding craftsmen
Prepare two tablets of stone for the covenant, speaking
Patiently, but with no hesitation,
No sense of the words being whipped from him, to his leaders:
"Thus I leave to you the duties of
Administering, of ordering, of judging.
The task which will long absorb my time,
My energy, and such poor brains as I have,
Will be the task of making the laws of our people,
The law you will administer. The law
Is like the blood channels of the body, or shall I say
That first there are the great trees of blood,
And then the numberless branches and twigs. It is the
Trunks that we must think of first, the solidities
Which even the weak of sight can see. The branches
And twigs can come later. First, we must remember
That the great laws come from God. They are laws for all men,
And yet they are laws the world has not seen before.
But I say this to you, that so long as men shall live—
In freedom, unoppressed—it is on such laws
That their lives must be based. They must know that
These laws are sanctified by the Lord himself,
And they must see the ground from which the great trees spring
As the godhead that sustains them. God is not a
Demon of the rivers, or of fire or air.
He is not a stone idol—He is a spirit,

And it is as spirit that men must worship him.
So there shall be no making of gods of stone
Or wood or iron or silver. Nor shall the name of God
Be thrown in the air like a ball or kicked like a pebble.
The very name is sacred and its use shall be sacred.
The day of rest, which is God's day, shall be sacred—
Given to the contemplation of the eternal,
While the body rests from labor. It shall be a day
For the family, and the family itself
Shall be seen on that day as sacred. Nay, the family
And the bond of marriage, and the children that are
The fruit of that bond, shall always be bound in a garland
Of love and honor. And what a man owns shall be sacred,
Since it comes from God—be it his goods or his life.
Both are inviolate—no killing, no stealing. Nay, more:
No coveting of the things our brothers possess,
For sin begins in desire. Above all, we are free,
Free beings, copies of that God
Who is the first and last free being—free
Even to choose to enter the covenant
With him, with him who made us. And now I ask:
'Will you accept the covenant?' " And again he asked
Not the leaders alone but all the people:
"Will you accept the covenant?" The word bounced,
Echoed—*covenant covenant*—and the reply
Echoed and bounced all along the valley.
The tablets in his arms, the graver's tools
In the hands of Joshua, who was to be with him
The long time of his absence, Moses began
To climb the mountain, slowly, Joshua after,
And the Israelites watched him leave—for how long?—their lives.
But Aaron was with them, Aaron still, in Aaron's hands
The rule, in Aaron's head the law, on Aaron's
Tongue the word. They watched, and Aaron watched,
Till Moses was lost to view, then turned to their lives,
Their grumbling wives, the cow in labor, sheep
With foot-rot, work and sleep, the common lot,
Thinking of God and Moses and the covenant
But not too much, having other things to do.

10 A RESTIVE PEOPLE

Up high on Horeb, with the evening coming on,
They looked at the rolling cloud that, somehow, beckoned,
And Moses nodded slowly, saying to Joshua:
"I must enter now. Do you understand? I must be
Entirely alone with the voice of all things. Make your
Camp somewhere down there, in the rocks' shelter."
And Joshua asked: "How long will it be?" Moses smiled.
"The world and the seas and the stars were made in
Six days. To make laws for the Israelites
May take somewhat longer. A good deal longer.
But I think we are well enough supplied." Joshua said:
"It will be a bread and water matter."—"Bread and water
Will suffice me. At dawn and at sundown.
But you are a young man. Hunt by all means,
But do not wander too far. Remember—if all this
Should be too much for me—if—" But Joshua said:
"You are not to talk in that manner." And Moses: "I
Grow aware of my age. The laws of living and dying
Will not be suspended for a mere
Instrument of the Lord. There will be others.
Already this one shows signs of wear. Remember,
I say, that you are the next chosen."—"No," said Joshua,
"There must be others before me—your brother—"
"Aaron," said Moses, "grows old too. And—I may say this,
The faith wavers in the old and the aging. They
Dream too much of the past, a past of old gods.
I must look to the young. To you. And now—"

Joshua saw the solemnity of the moment
And sank to his knees. Moses blessed him, saying:
"May your young body be washed in the waters of the eternal,
May the eternal dwell in muscle, nerve, sinew.
Be near, Joshua, near, for you too are called."
So Moses entered the cloud and was lost to view.
But Joshua, in moonlight, tending his fire, hearing
Owls and the bark and squeal of hunter and hunted,
Heard also a voice, and it was not the voice of Moses.
"It is true," he whispered to the fire. "All is true."
So time passed, and a time passed below
Among the Israelites neither exciting nor exacting,
Feeding their flocks and their children, baking bread,
Loving, quarreling, sitting at night around fires,
Talking of the past not the future. One such night,
Aaron and Koreh strolled among the tents
On an informal patrol when a voice hailed them
With "Any news from up there?" It was Dathan,
A little drunk, stepping out of the shadows.
"News?" said Aaron. And Dathan: "I apologize.
A very homely and earthy word. What news
Of the cow in calf? What news
Of the woman stoned by the well for alleged adultery?
I merely wondered—well, when he is returning to us.
It seems to be already a long time—"
"Two Sabbaths," said Koreh, "if you would be precise.
One of which, you will recall, you neglected to keep—"
"I forgot," said Dathan. "You will remember that I said I forgot.
You will also remember that I said I thought it was nonsense—"
"And that you were rebuked for blasphemy," said Aaron.
"The Lord's Day is not be be termed nonsense—"
"I thought we were all free men now," Dathan said,
"All entitled to a free opinion. Rebuked, indeed,
For blasphemy, indeed. Who says it's blasphemy?
You? Him?" And Koreh: "You should be sleepy, Dathan,
Not ready for argument. Go to your bed now."
And Dathan: "When I wish, sir. When I am ready.
Or is there a law about going to bed?" Aaron answered:
"Do not sneer at the law. The law is your

Tent and your blanket. The law watches over you
While you sleep."—"Pretty words," Dathan sneered,
"But tell me this: where is this law you sing about?
Is it written in books? Is it engraved on stone?
I hear much of the law but see nothing of it—"
"All in good time," said Koreh. "You will see
All that you wish to see. The law on stone
Will soon come down from that mountain. Then, Dathan,
You can pore over the law to your heart's content—"
"I wonder," Dathan said. "Is that blasphemy too?
Blasphemy to wonder whether he'll ever come down again?
He's growing old and weak: the wolves could get him.
His heart could stop. He may have received new orders:
*Go down, Moses, to the other side. There are
Other slaves to bring to freedom.*" Aaron frowned.
"Have a care, Dathan. You do not know what you are saying."
"Ah, more blasphemy, is it?" Dathan said.
"More lawbreaking? I'd be glad to see that law
Written down somewhere. And now I shall go to bed,
Like a good law-abiding citizen. God watch over you."
And he stumbled off in the shadows. Aaron and Koreh
Looked at each other. Aaron shrugged. The two
Continued their patrol. The next day came
With the things it had to bring—sheep to pasture,
A cow calving, a human child brought forth
And, that night, to the blowing of bull's horns
And the plucking of the harp and the breathing of the flute,
A celebratory song from Miriam, a dance from the maidens,
Extolling their God of life:

> His strength is the strength of the bull that charges
>   in thunder,
> His wonder is in the flow of the seed of men.
> Again and again, above in the skies and under
> The skies, in the gold noon and the moon's gold,
> His power and his wonder are told.
> Halleluiah halleluiah.

Outside their tent, in fireglow, Eliseba,
The wife of Aaron, spoke to Aaron: "So no news."
"As I have said before," said Aaron, "we do not

Talk of news."—"I thought perhaps Joshua
Might have come down—with news, or whatever I am to call it."
"Joshua has his orders."—"And you have yours—"
"And I have mine," said Aaron. "Orders to give orders.
My order was to keep order. Which I am doing—"
"Yes," said Eliseba, "which you are doing—"
"You have some strange thought in that head of yours,"
Aaron smiled, and she said: "No strange thought.
A very natural thought. You keep order
Until Joshua is ready to come from that mountain.
Then Joshua keeps order."—"But this is nonsense,"
Aaron said. "Joshua has his work. I have mine—"
"Whatever it is," she said, and he: "I am his voice.
Joshua is his right arm. That has been understood,
Clearly, ever since the war."—"War?" she said,
In feigned puzzlement. "Oh, the little desert skirmish
With those unwashed desert people. General Joshua.
Joshua the great warrior."—"Joshua," Aaron said,
"Is a good man and a good leader. Believe me,
We shall need good military leaders before that time comes
When we settle down in peace. What have you against him?'
"Nothing," Eliseba said. "I just wonder sometimes
How I fit in— How you, I mean—" He was stern, saying:
"What you mean, I think, is that you have not been
Accorded the respect you consider your due.
You want the deference you consider owing
To the wife of a great man. The *consort*
Of a great man. Did I ever pretend to be
A great man? There are no great men here,
Believe me. Not even my brother. He is under orders
More than anyone. He was thrown into that position
Against his will. Against his will, do you understand?
We ask very little. To build our nation. That means
Law, law and more law. What we are doing
Is waiting for that law to be hammered out,
Painfully. When we have law we will have judges.
I shall be a judge—is that great enough for you?
Eliseba, the Judge's wife. Will that do?"
But she said: "You misunderstand me. You

Misunderstand my meaning. Ah, I am not even sure
I understand it myself. But, let me say this:
Once there seemed so much to look forward to.
Now there seems to be nothing."—"Nothing?" he cried.
"Nothing to come out of Egypt a free people,
Free, I say. Nothing the wonders, miracles?"
"Miracles," Eliseba echoed. "Or is it trickery?
There are some who are saying it was trickery,
His trickery. That he knew a strong wind
Would blow back the waters. It's happened before, they say
And the water in those rocks, and the quails, the manna.
Cunning, clever—but it was all supposed to be
The power of this God. His God. And where is this God?"
"You forget," said Aaron wearily, "the miracles in Egypt.
God was in those, God is in everything—
In the strength of the wind and the lightning and the sea.
And now he talks to my own brother, gives him the law,
Makes a covenant with our people. Beware,
Beware of blasphemy, woman." Eliseba, unabashed,
Said: "You say that to everyone. And now you say it
To your own wife. Blasphemy blasphemy blasphemy.
But what I say is this: What comes next?
We move on to some other place full of sheep,
After General Joshua has kindly won more battles for us,
And then we obey the law, smelling of sheep dung.
Is that life?" Aaron said: "We are the builders.
We are the beginners. We will make kingdoms
Greater than Egypt when the time comes. But
That time is not yet." And Eliseba answered:
"We will look up at the sky, pretending we see
A God who is not really there—who only lives
In the mind of your brother Moses. Have you even thought
That your brother may be mad—that he'll starve to death
Up there, brooding on his God? And that we have to wait
While he starves to death or wanders away on the
Other side of the mountain, forgetting us,
All the big promises. Not that they are so big,
Those big promises. Looking after sheep
And bearing children and having lots of laws

And an invisible God grumbling all the time—"
"I think," said Aaron sighing, "we should go to bed—"
"Bed," said Eliseba. "Bed and work and bread
And goat's milk. And occasionally, if we are good,
A song and dance from your sister Miriam. Life.
At least in Egypt there was—ah, it is no matter—"
"In Egypt," Aaron cried, "there was misery,
Whips and pyramids and filthy stone idols. Misery—"
"Also," she said, "baked Nile fish and palm wine.
What are you going to do, Aaron—
Aaron of the golden mouth, what are you going
To do? The people are unhappy, Aaron."
"They have no right," he muttered, "to be unhappy.
They must be patient. Patience, the great thing is patience."
"And where did patience," she said, "ever lead them?
What did patience ever get them? They want to live.
He may never come back, Aaron of the golden mouth.
What are you going to do? This is your kingdom."
So she left him alone by the fire and he looked
Bitterly after her. *They want to live.*
Next day a strange thing, a new thing, though small.
One of the idle appeared before the children
With little figures of stone, crudely carved,
And a crude platform of wood, and he set the figures
Acting on that stage, lending them his voices,
One voice a mouse squeak, the other heavy, solemn,
A *bearded* voice, which rumbled: "Tell them all
That nobody is to work on the Sabbath, the Sabbath
Being my day, my day."—"Why not give us that day
And you have all the others? Then we should be able
To rest nearly all the time." The children laughed.
"Because," in thunder, "I tell you. And you tell them
That if they do wrong I will punish them, punish them—"
"How will you punish them?"—"I'll swoop down from on high
Like a mountain lion. I'll crash like a thunderbolt."
And one of the bolder children grasped the God-effigy
And chased the weaker with it, crying: "Go on,
On your knees, bow down, bow down or I will
Clout you on the head." And a sickly child,

Grinning, abased himself to joyful laughter.
But then a voice of true anger, Koreh's, crying:
"Stop! Stop that!" Surprised but unabashed,
The puppeteer and the children: what wrong had they done?
Here came some official spoilsport. Koreh said:
"You know the law. You know that there is to be no
Worshipping of graven images. And that means also
The pretense of worshipping—" The puppeteer cried back:
"Are there to be no children's games then any more?"
"I admit," admitted Koreh, "that the line is
Hard to draw. It will be drawn firmly when
He comes down. Meanwhile remember
What you have already been taught—that there is
Danger even in children's play." And he took the
Crude God of stone and hurled it, hurled it,
And the children looked at him with open mouths.
The law was a problem everywhere, on every level,
As Aaron found with the thieves arraigned before him,
Saying, calmly, clearly: "I am saying
Not that you stole as men steal in the
General way, the old way—from other men,
From this man or from that man—do you follow me?
But that you stole from us all. The gold and silver
And jewels that the Egyptians gave to us,
Gave us to go away—do you follow me?
Are the wealth not of one man, of one family,
Of one tribe, but of the entire people,
Of what we now call Israel." And the first thief,
Walleyed and hulking, said: "What you're saying then
Is that we stole from ourselves. But how can people
Steal from themselves? Answer me that." And Aaron:
"Listen carefully. Listen. A whole nation
Can own a thing in common—do you follow me?
Perhaps some public monument, some statue—"
"Some god, you mean?" said the second thief, a youth
Golden, angelic. And Aaron: "I did not say that.
Some fine piece of craftsman's work, shall we say,
That is set up in a public place, that would be
Seen and enjoyed by the whole people. It would be theft

For one man or three men to remove it. Now do you
Follow me?" But the first thief said: "That gold,
Silver and stuff was shut away in a wagon,
And not very well guarded, if I may say so.
Anybody could have taken some, but it happened to be
Us. And it happened that one of these Midianites
Didn't keep his mouth shut." Aaron turned to Caleb:
"Not very well guarded, do you hear?" And to the thieves:
"What have the Midianites to do with it?" The third thief said,
An upright clipped man, like a warrior:
"They wanted to sell us palm wine. As for us,
We wanted to buy it. We had nothing to buy it with.
Except sheep. But they said they had plenty of those—"
"I see," sighed Aaron. "Caleb, sequester the palm wine.
It belongs to the community. There may sometime
Be occasion to celebrate something. As for you three—"
And then he cried out in impotence: "Punishment, punishment—
What punishment can we give? By rights you should each
Have a hand cut off at the wrist. But who would be so
Foul as to order such bloody execution
And who so depraved as to do it? Nor can you be
Cast into prison. We are not a township—
We have no prisons. Throw you back to the wilderness?
That would be death, and theft hardly warrants it.
All I can say is that you must abide the
Coming of the covenant, the return of the
Ordained lawgiver. Be warned. You are free to go."
So they went, and the voice of the clipped and upright
Warrior-looking thief could be heard some way off,
Mimicking Aaron, while the others laughed.
"If I may speak," said Caleb— "Speak by all means,"
Aaron said, and Caleb: "We have here a nation
Of town-dwellers who have almost forgotten
That their forebears were herdsmen. It is hard to turn them
        so quickly
Into tenders of sheep again. They think of enslaving Egypt
As a land of fair cities. What have they, after all, here?
Goat's cheese and sheep fat and that useless glittering hoard
Out of a fair land of fine craft and richness.

Melt it down." And Aaron started at that.
"Melt it down," said Caleb. "We have men here wasted—
Men who have learned the crafts of smith and carver,
Brought down to be mere shepherds. Melt the gold
And melt the silver and give them work to do.
Some effigy of skill and beauty that shall
Stand in the midst of the encampment. Some symbol of
The unity of a people." Aaron shook his head:
"But this is no time for that. We are still watiting
To go to the land we are promised, there to build our
Cities and fill them full of the craftsman's work.
This is a time between times, it is not yet
Even an era of making. Except for the law,
The law first. We build first with law
And then out of stone and marble and metal—"
"A very long time of waiting," Caleb said.
"To many it feels that this is to be their life—
A life full of toil with nothing at all to look at
Save that sky and that mountain. He has been
A long time up that mountain. If, of course, he is
Still there." Glumly, both looked up
At the mountain. *If he is still there.*
"Even he said that," said Aaron to Eliseba,
The following dawn, as they lay hearing the cockcrow
And smelt the baking of bread. "Even Caleb.
The people are wavering, full of doubt. Some of them
Talk with regret of leaving Egypt. They forget so quickly.
They forget Moses. *If he is still there*, he said—"
"Whether he is there or not," Eliseba replied,
"You are here, you. The time is come, I think,
For you to rule."—"I do what I can," said Aaron—
"And what you can do is to say either *no* or *wait*.
No more. Have they been asking you for gods?"
"For what?" Aaron was startled. "For gods, gods,"
She said. "Not some big bearded father
Up the mountain or in the sky. Gods such as
The Egyptians have. Gods they can touch and speak to
And chide and beat if they do not behave well—"
"They are foolish," Aaron said. "They do not realize

How far we have come. We, of all the people of the earth,
Know what God is. Not gods—God—
The one containing the many. It is staggering.
Too staggering. Yes, they have been asking for
Gods."—"And what," said Eliseba, "do you say to them?
Wait, I will tell you. You thunder and use big words.
You talk of the big invisible God who has brought us
Out of Egypt and into the bondage of sheep dung.
And they don't understand."—"He will make them understand,
My brother." She said: "You used to be the great explainer.
He was supposed to be slow of speech. Well, talking
Is not enough now. What are you going
To do?" Roused, he cried: "Will *you* understand
What I say now? I will show them what God is,
Not talk and explain, but show. They need an
Image for their poor minds to cling to. They must
See the strength of God. He carries the sun and the moon
On his brow. He has the power of all of the
Beasts of the earth and yet he is gentle, loving.
But that is not God: it is but a picture of God—"
"Time to get up," she said. "You have ruling to do."
So that very morning the treasure hoard swung open,
And the gold and silver and jewels of the Israelites
Were brought in baskets joyously while Aaron explained
To the craftsmen and artists what was to be made. One art,
The art of song, was fired while the kiln was built
And the fire puffed within it, and the song was sung
By the people, joyous, their eyes at last to be fed
With something other than promises:

> His head is the sun,
> He carries the moon on his brow,
> His limbs are the north, the west,
> The east, the south,
> And his breath the winds thereof.
> His coat is speckled with the stars.
> He strides in power over all the world.
> Halleluiah halleluiah.

11 | THE GOLDEN CALF

OUT of the fire came an indeterminate lump
Of fused gold and silver, but mostly gold,
And the craftsmen worked on it: it became
An indeterminate beast with a crescent moon
On its brow like horns, so that a certain child
Cried: "That's it—that's what I saw—that time
When we walked through the water—up in the sky it was,
A baby bull." The father said: "A calf, you mean,
A bull calf. I see. Like that, was it? A heavenly bull calf
And the parents smiled at each other: *Children.* Soon
On a rough tumulus the image was ready to be raised
And blocked into place with stone. Aaron was there,
And Aaron spoke to the people who watched, saying: "Listen,
Children of Israel, you have asked for gods.
You were wrong to do so, sinful indeed, but the sin
Sprang mostly from ignorance and from inability
To grasp what great thing has happened to us." (The craftsmen
Polished the back, the horns, the blunt muzzle.) "For what
      has happened
Is this: we have been chosen by God himself
—Not by gods, not even by a king of gods, but by God,
The one true indivisible God who made us
And made everything. At this moment my brother Moses,
Our leader, our giver of laws, is in converse with the
Voice of God on the mountaintop. The voice he hears
Is perhaps his own voice, animated by God,
For God has no voice as a man has a voice. God

Has no body, God is in no one place.
God is spirit, and spirit is unshackled by the
Chains of time and space. God is everywhere.
The image you see before you is not God—
The very idea is absurd. But it will serve
To remind you of God, each day as you pass it. God
Is strength, and this is an image of strength—its head
The sun, the moon on its forehead, its limbs the four
Corners of the world. But it is a loving strength,
A mild strength, the strength of an eternal being
That will never use its strength against us." The child cried:
"A bull calf, that's what it is," and the people smiled.
And Aaron smiled, saying: "It is not what it looks like
That is important. What is important is that you
See in it an image of our unity as a people
Chosen by the one true God. At last the silver and gold
Of the Egyptians who enslaved us have been put to
Holy use—the profane made holy, remember that.
What was hidden away is now here to be seen by all
—The richness of a people's unity—" (And now there were
        jewels for eyes)
"And the ultimate unthinkable richness of God himself,
Whose silver is the moon, whose gold the sun,
Whose jewels the eternal constellations of heaven."
He smiled at the applause, but Miriam,
Standing near with her children, did not smile,
Nor smiled when, in huge moonlight, the young danced about it
Singing:

> Where will our wedding breakfast be?
> Up in the fronds of a dikla tree.
> What will we drink? What will we eat?
> The moon for wine and the sun for meat.

And the old sat by, approving, a bit of life in the evening
Now. "It has become the center of life," smiled Aaron.
"A gathering place for talk and play. It is as if we were
Building a city." But Miriam said: "Not for long,
Not that for long. I saw some old men this morning
Touching it for luck, as they said. And there was a

Young man giving thanks."—"It is good to give thanks,"
Said Aaron—"Thanks to an image?" Miriam said.
"His wish had come true, something to do with a girl,
And he said that thing was magical."—"Harmless, Miriam,
Harmless. A simple people needs something simple
To feed its senses."—"Wait," said Miriam. "Wait."
And one evening the moon still huge, Dathan and his wife
Sat drinking palm wine, the three thieves with them, and he said:
"Can you get any more of this stuff?"—"What do we
     buy it with?"
Said the walleyed one. "That chunk of gold up there?"
"Risky," said the angelic one. "I somehow doubt
That you'd get away with it."—"Well," Dathan said,
"I'd rather drink this than drink that smoke that the
Young ones drink, snuff up rather, that grass that grows
By the well. Visions of golden cities,
That's what it's said to give you. Men of my age,
It makes us sick." Dathan's wife tipsily sang:
"Where will our wedding breakfast be?"—"I'd rather,"
Dathan said, "drink this than take that smoke stuff—"
"Some of the tribe of Judah," said the soldierly thief,
"Mash up dates and add honey and water. It bubbles,
Bubbles, you know."—"I suppose it's against the law,"
Said the angelic thief, his gold hair moon-ensilvered.
"Nothing," Dathan said, "is against the law,
Because there is no law. It has to be written down,
Then it becomes law. Not that anybody can read it,
Except those that pretend they can. The bondage
Of unintelligible signs. That is well put,
Remember that." And Dathan's wife went: "Unin-
Telligibubble."—"He's coming down soon,"
Said the soldierly thief.—"Who says so?" Dathan asked.
"Only a rumor," said the thief. "Still, I suppose it's
Time we knew where we stood. Then we get the law—"
"We ought to have a sort of celebration,"
Dathan said, "not when he gets here, but before.
I suppose he'll have a law against celebrations,
All nicely carved out."—"What will we celebrate?"
Asked the angel.—"Oh, said Dathan, "we'll think of

Something or other."—"Rother," giggled his wife.
But it was not till the new moon that something or other
Got into the people, helped by palm wine, date wine.
Some drunken women were singing Miriam's song
About the effigy:

> His strength is the strength of the bull that charges
> in thunder,
> His wonder is in the flow of the seed of men.
> Again and again, above in the sky and under
> The sky, in gold noon and the moon's gold,
> His power and wonder are told.
> Halleliuah halleliuah.

Some of the young sang their marriage song, and others
Drank smoke, while some of their elders kept to palm wine,
Date wine. All very harmless: the young dancing about
The effigy, the old clapping their hands
To the rough music. Harmless enough perhaps
The fixing, by drunken women, of a crude phallus,
A chunk of rolled leather, to the effigy's loins,
And Dathan swaying grinning with a pair of pomegranates.
But then the calf was jerked, to cheers, from its plinth,
Brought down to strong young shoulders, carried about
In song, while the tremulous old touched it, praying
For an end of the journey, for all to go well. Song
And a claw-buttock dance behind it, one young girl
Shedding her garments one by one in the dance,
Then seized by two young men, screaming and laughing.
Aaron and Miriam were far from all this, tending
A sick child in a distant tent, Aaron saying
(And the child was the child who had had the vision)
        to the mother:
"The fever must come to its height. And then, we hope,
He will grow cool again. Give him nothing to drink
But bathe his forehead."—"Listen," Miriam said.
He listened, both listened. "So," she said, "it is come.
God help us." They hurried, meeting on the way
Grave members of the tribe of Levi: *"We can do
Nothing. We always knew it was a
Grave mistake. Graven images.* Aaron saw,

Miriam saw a woman, near naked, on the ground,
And the calf's phallus in pretended hammering rut,
The calf in strong arms, and cheers and cheers,
The old, clawing buttocks, dancing, men and women,
Men and men, in a dance mime of sodomy,
The young, mad on the smoke they had drunk, dancing
Crazed dances of their own, a hugely corpulent
Sot draining, to cheers, a carboy of palm wine,
And Caleb, crying for order, sense, near-trampled,
And other Levites brutally stricken with staves.
"God help us," Miriam said. "You see what it is—
They are back to the worship of— Wasted, all wasted."
"I will speak to them," Aaron said. "Let me mount the
Plinth." (Was that woman Zipporah, was that
Zipporah?) An obese matron, naked,
Pig-squealed, pleasured by a skeletal youth. Aaron smote,
Smote with his stave, mounting. "Listen," he cried.
"Listen." And a few turned and groaned and cheered.
"Brothers and sisters—children of Israel—listen.
Return to your dwellings at once, under pain of death.
Sin, sin—the Lord sees—the Lord will strike." Cheers,
And many were swift to drag him down, drowning his shouts,
Stripped him, thrust a jug of wine to his
Shouting mouth, dragged him into the throng.
(Far above, on Horeb, Joshua,
Tending his night fire, thought he heard reveling,
Riot, war. He turned to the cloud, heard a
Stronger noise of hammer and chisel on stone,
And a kind of—or did he imagine it only?—
Disheartened thunder.) Dancing, rutting,
The disrobing of a screaming boy by men who
Slavered in lust. Lust, drunken fighting,
And Dathan, drunk, screaming ecstatic: "There has to be
A sacrifice, the god wants a sacrifice," pointing
Among cheers and growls to a trembling girl. Miriam
Stood in Aaron's place, hardly heard: "Cannot you
Understand? This is another kind of
Slavery. God, the true God, sees all and will punish
Terribly. Turn away from your sin before it is

Too late." A cloud covered the thin moon,
And some, in slow fear, looked up. "A sign," she cried.
Then the cloud passed. "Cease your wickedness.
God will forgive, God will understand." But they
Dragged her down, stripping and beating her, lifting
The battered dull gold effigy to its old place,
Holding the terrified naked girl beneath
On a jagged slab, while a hulking lout as priest
Prayed gibberish to the calf—*O guk O guk*
Bondage of unintelligibubble. Gaaaaaar!
And he raised the knife and plunged, plunged
Till he was tired of plunging. Horror, awe,
Joy. He covered his arms and head with blood,
He daubed the loins of the calf in it, and now
The crowd surged about, dipping in blood,
Anointing their own loins. They brought a boy,
Already stunned with a sharp rock, and rent him,
And some drank the blood and chewed and spat out
The rent flesh. (A drunk made slobbering love
To a woman equally drunk, and, equally drunk,
Another man wrestled with him in jealousy
And then took a stone and spilled his brains.
All brains and blood about them, he and she
Made slobbering love.) The dull gold effigy
Was everywhere daubed with blood and brains and seed
And, like red seed, blood dripped from its loins.
Battered and sobbing, Miriam crawled to her tent
And found Eliseba there, and the children, safe,
But where was Zipporah? The moon was setting.
The faintest dawn-streak flushed. And high on Horeb
Moses emerged from the cloud, under his arms
Two tablets, intricately carved, grim, growing gentle
As he bade the sleeping Joshua awake.
Joshua looked up, saw the tablets, saw
A kind of white light about the head of Moses,
And, seeing, knelt. "Rise, Joshua," he was told.
"We have mischief below. We must go down to the mischief."
So they descended as dawn grew, till at length,
From a ridge above the encampment, they saw enough:

A beast of metal drunkenly on a plinth,
Daubed with dried blood, some of it flaking off,
A naked body, too mauled to show its sex,
Men and women sleeping naked, corpses,
Blood everywhere, odd whimpering cries
From sources unseen, a half-devoured whole sheep,
The flies already at their work, shattered wine jugs,
Blood. "Call," said Moses quietly. "Call, Joshua."
So Joshua put his hollowed hands to his cheeks
And called a long sound. He called and called.
Some stirred, then slept again, moaning. Some
Stirred and listened and wondered, dazed, then saw
Dried blood in the sun. Miriam heard,
Ceasing to sob, and Aaron, bruised, dry blood on him,
Heard. Many heard, looking up in fear, and wonder,
Seeing bones, spilt wine, soon silent in the camp,
Two men walking. Zipporah, lying alone,
Blood on her garment, saw: light from his head,
His, shining, and behind his head an instant
The battered horns. He did not seem to see her.
Then Aaron stood before Moses, saying nothing,
Having nothing to say, then fell down in tears,
And Moses said, in sadness: "Not enough knowledge.
Never enough. And out of ignorance, evil.
The work wasted. All the work wasted."
In his arms were the stones, painfully chiseled.
"The covenant is broken. We must start again."
And soon to an assembled nation, weeping and fearful:
"The covenant is broken. We must start again.
You said you would accept the covenant.
But you had no faith, a frail and ignorant people.
And now the tablets of the law, so lovingly,
So painfully inscribed, must be smashed to dust.
For what was accepted in freedom was rejected in freedom.
Men are born free to do good and free to do ill.
You chose the latter way. You must suffer for that,
Suffer, since freedom always has its price.
You must suffer for that, in modes of suffering
That soon you will see, hear, smell, taste, feel in the

Very nerve and the very marrow. But first
We must perform the rite of the breaking of the covenant.
So be it." And he threw the stones to the earth.
Aaron and Koreh took stones and broke the stones,
Ground the stones to dust, sweating. The words
Were released to the sphere of the spirit, but the stone
Was dust. "We must start again," said Moses.
"Once more I ascend the mountain, there to take
Once more counsel of the Lord our God, but first—"
It was evening, and a great fire was being blown
To white heat. "What you worshipped," Moses cried,
"Must be your bane. The thing you took unto yourselves
In the spirit you must now in chastisement take
Unto yourselves in the flesh. Not all, but some.
For you are all one people, and it suffices
That one limb, tooth, nerve, eyeball be enforced
To shriek out for the entire body to know
Pain. Pain. I have appointed officers
Of the tribe of Levi to see that mouths which cried
In obscene ecstasy shall now, in a diverse mode,
Cry out. Not all but some, the grosser sinners.
What you kissed you now must eat and drink."
The calf on its plinth was dragged down by the Levites
And cast into the fire, there to dissolve
To a scalding broth. "This," he cried, "was your God."
It was mingled with water and thrust down the sinners' throats.
Nor was this all. The grosser sinners were stoned,
Hanged, pierced by arrows, hurled from the slopes
(But not Dathan, whose destiny lay otherwise,
Whose potency of grossness was, as it were,
Decreed as a thorn for Moses). The masons chose
New stone and shaped it for a new covenant.
And Moses, before he sought the peak of Horeb
Once more, Joshua with him, asked the people:
"Will you remember that this is the Lord your God,
Who brought you out of Egyptian bondage? Will you
Promise to worship no other God but Him,
Nor to make images of things that are on the earth
Or in the sky or rivers and seas for profane

And sinful worship? Will you keep the Sabbath holy,
Preserve the holiness of the family, honor your parents,
Respect the sanctity of the bond of marriage? Do you
Promise never to steal, never to murder,
Never to lust after what is another's? Will you
Keep the covenant the covenant will you
Keep the covenant?" *We will we will.*
The valley rang with shamed affirmation.
Yes hurtled through the air as the last of the
Condemned hurtled from the slopes. So Moses and Joshua
Climbed Horeb for the second time, leaving below
A chastened nation burying its dead,
Burying much else. So time passed, with the covenant
Unbroken, the covenant the sacred body of the law
Inscribed not in the riddling signs of the priests
They had known in Egypt but in a new way, a way
Apt for a covenant, with signs for sounds of speech,
That all might read if they would, but the sacred stones
Had to be housed in a sacred place. The craftsmen
Built an ark of wood, with beauty and cunning
Spent on it to the utmost, and here the covenant
Was tabernacled. Moses said to Aaron:
"It is in your keeping, Aaron. *Aaron the priest—*"
"The priest," Aaron said. "How must I take that?
In manner of a punishment?" But Moses said:
"A priest is God's voice. Could any man wish
To be higher than God's voice?"—"Once," Aaron said,
"I was your voice." —"And so," his brother replied,
"Take this not in manner of a punishment but in
Manner of a promotion." They looked at each other,
A curve unreadable on each other's lips.
And Aaron said: "Well then—to my first office."
And Moses: "God be with you, man of God."
So Aaron was enrobed and he walked to the ark
And reverently shut the covenant within,
Improvising a ceremony: "Hereon is inscribed
God's law. The very stone shall be accounted
Sacred. Behold, our God is a just God."
Stiff-jointed the people knelt. Then Moses knelt.

And Aaron the priest prayed: "God, who art a just God,
Be also, we beseech, a forgiving God.
For men are weak, being made but of earth's clay,
Quick to transgress. If, Lord, we have sinned once,
Will we not sin again? If we were perfect,
Would we have need of thee?" Moses, kneeling,
Was thoughtful (*weak—forgiving*). After sunset,
Zipporah, his wife, preparing Gershom, his son,
For sleep, heard Gershom's question once more:
"Is he still very busy?"—"Yes," she replied, "busy.
He has the whole of Israel to look after—"
"When," asked Gershom, "will he be with us again?"
But, before she could answer, a shadow stood between
His bed and the lamp of sheep fat. Gershom said:
"You had better not stay too long, sir. Israel needs you."
And Moses smiled and wept and took his wife
In trembling arms. "Who am I," trembling, "to reproach,
Even to talk of sin or weakness? To forgive
If forgiveness is needed—enough. Forgive me too,"
As she sobbed in his arms. "We all have to start again."
"It was little enough," she sobbed. "Wine in my head,
A pair of young arms in the dance. But it was too much—"
"Learning is hard," he said. "We all have to learn.
And now we can start again." There were family embraces,
Sobs, even laughter as Gershom said once more:
"Israel needs you. How long will you stay?"
But the time of staying under the mountain in the valley
Of Jethro was now to end. An order of march was worked out,
Moses drawing with his stave on the sandy earth,
Saying: "There in the midst the ark of the covenant,
With its own bodyguard drawn from the Levites. No enemy
Shall take it, no infidel defile it. It is our hub,
And, as twelve spokes, the fixed and changeless posts
Of the tribes," showing—Dan, Reuben, Benjamin . . .
"A battle order," Joshua said. And Moses:
"You may call it that." Then Caleb: "When do we march?"
And Moses pondered. "Miriam," he said to Aaron.
"How is she?" Aaron said: "Very sick. But ready.
Ready to go to the land." *She will not see it,*

Moses told himself. *But it is better thus,*
To die striving forward, in others' hope.
"So," he pronounced, "we move tomorrow at dawn."
There was weeping at the well when they took their leave
        of Jethro
And his daughters, some now married, some not. Weeping
Of many over many graves, brethren buried
Much else buried. Miriam, pale, wasted,
Lay in rugs on an oxcart, Eliseba tending her.
Just before the raising of the staff as signal, incorrigible
Dathan rooted in the ashes of the punitive fire
And came up with a thumbnail fragment of gold, holding
That nothingness up to the sun; the sun swallowed it.
They took their last look of Horeb, its peak no longer
Enmisted: eagles circled there. Towards rock,
Desert, thirst, hunger, the law in their midst,
They moved.

12 | DEATH AND THE LAW

At the next oasis Miriam's end drew near.
Moses wiped her fever, in the coolness of a cave,
And Miriam shuddered painfully, hearing from without
That marriage song of the young: "It will happen again.
Again." But Moses soothed her, saying: "This
Is a different excitement: they already smell
The air of our promised land, or think they do.
The hope lies with the young. The old, alas,
Are more than ever set in the old ways.
They have learned fear but not yet understanding.
And you, my sister, how is it with you?"
She murmured: "I lose blood. I am weak. But feel
Little pain. I shall be glad to move on.
Move on. No more. Towards something even if we
Never reach it."—"We shall reach it," he said.
"There's a hunger to build—especially with the young.
To build, say, a temple and then a city
To hold the temple." She said: "I will not see it,
But it matters little enough. My work, the work
I was ordained to do has been long done.
You were my work. My name perhaps will be known
For that. Girls given the name of Miriam.
It is something. I rescued a child from murderers.
And if I had not rescued that child—" He said:
"You were ordained to. It was all laid down.
We are all in God's pattern." But she, distressed:
"Was that too part of God's pattern? Is then evil

Part of God's pattern?"–"We must believe it," he said.
"If evil is in man it must come from his maker–"
"And it goes on," she said. 'It will go on.
Law will not quench it. I see much evil to come.
Law will not contain it. Nor will punishment–"
"But men," he insisted, "learn from their own transgressions.
There will be no more building of golden calves.
Other things perhaps–man is ingenious.
He gets his ingenuity from God."
And then she wept. "They had ceased to be men and women.
I could do nothing." Later her mind rambled
Or grew prophetic. "I heard the soldiers singing
Their dirty song. And God surely was there,
For if they had not been singing they would have heard,
Heard him crying. A newborn cry, very loud
In the night. But God made them sing their song,
Which was filthy and evil, and so they did not hear.
The river then and the bulrushes and the
Little floating cradle. Meant to live,
He was meant to live: 'Girl girl,' they said,
'Who are you, girl, can you get him a wet nurse, girl?'
And I did. Poor mother. But he lived, lived.
A pretty baby. They made him an Egyptian."
(The moon showed Passover, the angel passing over.
"Will he pass over tonight?" the children asked,
Making sour faces over the bitter herbs,
The hard dry bread.) "They would not see it," said Miriam.
"Many gods, like bits of pottery,
A housewife's pride, but not the one true God.
So simple, and so many thousands of years
For it to come to the light. And still they will not
See it. And when they see it they will say:
What good is it, what good? For the pains of life
Will not be easier. Truth makes nothing easier.
But truth must still be sought." Eliseba, hiding tears,
Said: "Rest, my dear, rest." But Miriam said:
"Oh, there will be no rest. And when it is built,
The city, it will be knocked down, and the temple
Destroyed with the city. And it will go on and on.

They will wander and be made to wander farther.
For there is no abiding city. Only the dark.
I must speak to my brother Moses." Moses said:
"I am here, Miriam." She said: "You will not see it.
You will be forbidden to see it. It will take a
Long time to be made clean." Then they waited
For Miriam to say more, but she said no more.
Her eyes were open, but said no more. And Aaron
Closed her eyes, and then the wailing began.
The angel, it was shuddered about the camp.
Aaron said: "Let the soul of this thy servant
Go calmly to its haven, where there is no pain,
Where the mill of the heart grinds no more
Of the bread of tribulation." Moses touched her face.
"Rest, Miriam, rest." Then left and went
Into the dark to weep. So they buried her—
Another grave to mark their journey. Buried her,
With rites according to the law of Israel.
Nothing stayed, but there was always the law . . .
And Moses was administering the law one day
When Caleb appeared to speak of a monstrous serpent
Voided from a child's body. "A bad omen.
That is the general feeling." But Moses said:
"Let us hear nothing of omens. Let us hear rather
Of foolishness. What has the child been eating?"
So the story came out: some of the Israelites,
Sick of their diet of mutton, trading a sheep
For a pig from a wandering tribe that herded pigs.
"The pig," said Moses, "is not like other beasts.
It harbors worms in its gut and gives the worms
To those who eat it. Call it an act of revenge,
Though posthumous." Nobody smiled. Loudly he said:
"Does it occur to one that this serpent
Is a consequence of eating forbidden flesh—
Not a sign from heaven, but the passing on
Of a disease from beast to man? Can they not *think?*
Are they to be treated forever like children?" Caleb said:
"There is no instruction about this. What is the law?
It seems not to be covered by the basic ten—"

"More laws," said Moses. "No food from now on may be eaten
Without some act of supervision, God help us.
We need priestly intervention even there.
The body of the law must wax fat
Because the brain of the Israelite is small.
They cannot eat, God help us, without being
Told what to eat. Shall we put the spoon to their mouths?"
And, on another day, when Aaron was called
To see a sick child, its loins inflamed,
And its parents applying some filth of fat and spittle,
He saw that the child was uncircumcised. "Dust," he said,
"Dirt has been trapped there." The father: "We did not think."
"You did not think," said Aaron. "And yet Zipporah,
Wife of our leader Moses, herself gave to God
As an offering the foreskin of her firstborn.
Was she not at that moment divinely inspired
To do what was for the child's good? We are, above all,
A people of cleanliness. Remember that.
We are not disease-ridden rats of the wilderness.
Your son shall be circumcised." But the mother said:
"I am not Zipporah. I could not take the knife
To my precious." Aaron sighed. "It shall be done for you.
All that is needful to be done for you shall be done.
So God be with you." And wearily he left.
But there was yet another day when Moses
Sat with his problems, in the cool of a cave,
And a tribal leader came with another problem,
A violation of the law of the Sabbath.
"What were they doing?" Moses wearily asked.
"Gathering palm fronds to feed a fire. It seemed
Harmless enough, but, knowing that the covenant
Is strict on this matter, knowing that you yourself—"
"Yes?" said Moses. "—Set great store by the
Punctilious observance of the Sabbath rest—"
"It is not just *I myself*," said Moses. "This
Punctilious observance, as you term it
Somewhat grandiloquently, is of the very
Essence of the law. It is to do with man's duty,
Duty, not right, to abstain from labor

That the body may be at peace and the spirit
At one with God. With God. One day in seven—
Can we not spare that day to honor our God?"
"This," said the tribal leader, "is generally
Recognized and accepted, but—after all,
The gathering of a few palm fronds—" "Yes?" said Moses—
"Well," said the leader, "we were somewhat unsure
Of an appropriate penalty. The men in question
Were, naturally, rebuked. But they did not seem to be
Truly repentant. And then what happened was—"
"Yes?" said Moses.—"What happened was that one of them
Was discovered later looking for dry sticks—
For tinder. The rebuke had been of no avail—"
"So now?" said Moses.—"Now I seek instruction.
As to the appropriate mode of punishment."
Then Moses felt the wrestling within
And the curse of his leadership was sour in his mouth,
But, wearily, hopelessly, he said: "The holy rest
Of the Sabbath may not be defiled. Let the miscreants
Be stoned to death." The tribal leader did not
Think that he . . . "Forgive me, I do not think that I
Quite—" And Moses: "My sentence was, I fancy,
Clearly enough articulated. Let the miscreants
Be stoned to death." The leader: "With respect and deference,
I do not think that my people could at all
Possibly accept such a harsh, disproportionate—
Forgive me. Sir." And Moses stood and said:
"Can you or can your people think of
An alternative punishment? More rebukes? Torture?
Turn them into living martyrs? Imprisonment?
We are all imprisoned till we reach the land.
Best be bold and have done with it. The law is the law,
One, indivisible. To kill another man
Merits death. But to kill the Lord's day,
The living breathing peace that belongs to the Lord,
Can that be accounted a lesser crime? The Lord God
Is thus blasphemed against. Blasphemy,
A sneer, a gob of spit in the face of God.
Let them be stoned to death." He said no more,

Returning to his rock seat and his problems,
But the tribal leader was aghast. That very day
The penalty was exacted—a walleyed thief,
A thief whose hair shone gold in the sun, transfixed
With twisted ropes to tree trunks, the crowd around
Murmuring, and soon doing more than murmur
When the muscles of the executioners
Glistened in sunlight. They took, in an easy rhythm,
Rock after rock from the pile and hurled,
Hurled. The first died quickly, faceless, but the other
Lasted till there was not much of the human about him,
And then his head dropped to his shoulder. Not murmurs,
But yells of anger before the cave of Moses,
And stones thrown. The armed guard held steady.
Justice not murder to hell with your commandments
Break your stone again murderer your laws are
Nothing but murder. Grim, he came out. The stones flew.
He bled from his brow. The guard hit back with staves.
Many dispersed, yelling, but Dathan and the
Third thief, the soldierly one, held their ground,
And, inside the cave, Dathan spoke of barbarism.
"Barbarism?" Moses said. "You talk to me of
Barbarism? When you, to my certain knowledge,
Were one of the leaders of the most filthy display
Of barbarism known in the annals of all the tribes.
Count yourself lucky, Dathan, that you were not chosen
For the ultimate punishment after that abomination
Which stinks still in God's nostrils." Dathan replied:
"Very well, Moses. If I was a sinner,
I was unenlightened. What excuse can you show?"
And Moses cried: "*Excuse*, Dathan? Must we
Have excuses to sustain the law,
The law that sustains the life of man? For I
Am in the service of life, while you are
All given over to death. You, the nay-sayer,
The sneerer, the denier, you still live,
While better than you could ever be granted a dream
Of becoming are struck down by your sneers,

Your greed and your lust." The soldierly thief said:
"It is a strange way of serving life,
Killing men. It was my brother you killed,
Do you know that? A man who had his faults,
Like all men, but meant no harm to any, dead
And dead like a dog beaten to pulp by children
Dead because of some nonsense about the Sabbath,
For nonsense it is, and all the world knows it for nonsense—"
"All the world," said Moses, "the little world
Of the stupid who disdain the vision. Your brother, you say.
On your head and the heads of the evil like you
Lies my sister's death. Ah, but it is no matter—"
"Ah, it comes clearer now," Dathan said, in glee.
"It is not the law that drives you—it is revenge—"
No, Dathan said Moses, "not revenge.
Vengeance is not for me. Vengeance is for
The Lord God, in his own time. There is for me
The law and the enforcing of the law—
Yes, by murder if need be, since you hold
That just execution is murder—until men
Cease to be ignorant and know that their own good
Is the good of the commonalty, and that that good
Is enshrined in the law. You will learn, be made to learn.
Perhaps you are already learning, you,
Dathan, the most obdurate of my children—"
'"Oh yes," sneered Dathan. "I am learning one thing:
Remember thou keep holy the Sabbath day."
In torment of spirit, Moses walked the night,
Addressing bitterly the torrent of stars
And the silence of the wildreness. "My people," he said.
        "Your people.
They are a stiff-necked people. They are a people
Who savor their ignorance like manna. Why why,
O Lord, am I set above them? Why, of all the
Men that walk the earth, was I chosen
To lead them to a fair land that is
None of their deserving? Why, Lord, was I chosen
To bring them to the law they despise and spurn?
They speak harshly of me, spit in my shadow,

Cast stones at my son, send my wife home weeping.
Am I not a man like any other,
Deserving of peace—deserving of wine at sundown,
A glowing fire to dream into under the stars?
Was I not better off as a prince in Egypt,
Jeweled with office, wearing the perfume
Of the respect and the worship of men? God, my Lord,
I speak from the heart as I have ever done.
I am sick to death of the burden of rule I bear.
What will you do if I renounce it now—
If I pass it to Aaron or to Joshua
Or to any of the young who promise richly?
You can do little more than strike me down
As you have struck down others. Well, it may be
That I am willing to be struck down—lie at peace
In the earth, where is no more trouble, pain
Or oppression of the wicked. I defy you, then,
Or am willing to do so, as others have.
Am I not free to do so? Am I not a man
Like other men, clothed in the garment
Of liberty of choice? And yet I have not forgotten
The humility of the servant before the master.
In humility I ask—let your servant
Go, let your servant go." But there was no answer
From the array of the stars or the night's silence.
So he went to his bed, finding his wife asleep,
His son happy in a dream, and tried to sleep.
Then he heard a voice, his own, grown old,
Speak slow and tired: "Moses, my servant Moses,
I will ride you as a horseman rides a horse.
You will always know my weight on your back,
My spurs in your flank. I will never let you go.
You have doubted, and you will doubt again and again,
But, in spite of your doubts, you will bear the burden
To life's end. You will lead your people to the land
That is promised, since that is my will. You will lead them,
But you yourself will never eat or drink
Of the fruit of the fulfillment of the promise.
I will never let you go, but I will never

Let you enter. Nor will any one
Of your generation, sick with the doubt
Of the Lord's promise, ever enter that land.
The milk of my beneficence and the honey
Of my jealous love—neither is for you
Nor for the generation that is yours.
Those will flow in a land you may see from afar
But whose soil will never bless your foot, whose air
Never delight your nostrils, and whose sun
Never warm your gray head. I have spoken."
Gershom lay silently awake now, listening
In wonder to a sound he had never heard:
The sobbing of his father.
                              So at daybreak
They addressed themselves to the march, with Moses grim
In the vanguard, and the young, guarding the tablets,
Sang with a hope they had a right to feel:

> We go to the land
> Where the hand of the Lord
> Showers blessing, and
> The sun fails not, nor the soil
> And man's toil is a prayer
> Of thankfulness to the Lord.
> There it lies, beyond our eyes
> And yet within reach of our hand.
> We go to the unknown land.
>   Lustily singing,
The young, guarding the Ark of the Covenant.

13 | EVER UNREST

THE wilderness of Paran. Wilderness
After wilderness, and now this wilderness.
Sand, rock, distant mountain. A copper sun
Riding a wilderness of bronze. Thirst,
Their close companion in the wilderness.
Here? Here? they cried. *We camp here?*
A wife said humbly: "I should think there must be
A good reason for it. I have a feeling—"
What feeling, woman? "There must be a reason.
What are they doing up there?" Pointing
Into the distance, and they squinted into
The distance, to the mountain range,
To two lone figures, high up, scanning the distance.
Moses pointed afar. "Is that Canaan?"
Aaron asked. "It is what I saw in my dream,"
Said Moses. "I heard the name." What Aaron saw
Was wilderness and mountain. "Now," said Moses,
"We must spy out the land. There will be a long
Time of waiting still. Set up the tabernacle.
Our symbol of permanency." Aaron groaned:
"Permanency. What do we live on?" *What do we live on?*
They asked that question down in the wilderness,
Setting up their tents. One man said to another:
"Can *you* see anything beyond there?"
"The same as lies beyond *there*—the way we came—"
"Then what is all the fuss about?"—"He says
We're near it. But we've been near it

Ever since we left Egypt. It's always the same.
Sand sand sand and more sand—"
"Be reasonable. We have rocks as well, sometimes."
And, in mock solemnity, the other intoned:
"Beyond there, O my people, lieth Canaan.
And what is Canaan?" Another growled: "It's a word
Meaning a dry throttle and an empty gut.
And sand, of course." He spat towards the sand.
The sun and sand wrestled for the moisture
And the sand won. In the midst of the encampment
The ark of the covenant, magnificently adorned,
(*Nothing too good for the law*, they growled) shone out,
And artists still worked on its adorning. Aaron
Called out the names of those who were to spy
Into the wilderness ahead, one from each tribe:
"Shammua, son of Zaccur, from the tribe of Reuben.
Shaphat, son of Hori, from the tribe of Simeon.
Caleb, son of Jephunneh, from the tribe of Judah.
Igal, son of Joseph, from the tribe of Issachar.
Joshua, son of Nun, from the tribe of Ephraim.
Palti, son of Raphu, from the tribe of Benjamin.
Gaddiel, son of Sodi, from the tribe of Zebulun."
And so to the end of the twelve. Moses addressed them:
"Over there, my sons—the land of Canaan.
Yes, the promised land. But a land so fertile
That it is doubtless inhabited by men
Of rich flesh and strong bone. Yet remember:
Whoever now possesses the land possesses it
Not by God's promise. You will find people wild,
        uncircumcised,
Worshipping idols. The land is ours,
But not ours for the easy taking. Your task
Is to spy out the land." They listened, alert.
"Get you up this way southward and go up
Into the mountain, and see the land, what it is.
Whether it is fat or lean, whether there is timber
Or not. And be of good courage, my children,
And bring of the fruit of the land." In his tent, near dawn,
Joshua lay with a girl, who said: "How long?"

"Who knows?" he answered. "—But you will be back?"
"Again, who knows? But you will be a good reason
For wanting to come back," embracing her.
"Why," she asked, "is it you who have to go?
I thought you were learning to stand in his place—"
"He would go himself," said Joshua, "if he were younger.
He's as curious as I am." The girl pouted:
"That is the trouble with men. Too much curiosity.
Never at rest." He kissed her. "—You are my rest,
You are my heart's ease, my soul's tranquillity—"
"But curiosity comes first," she said. "—Alas,
Daybreak," and he gave her a final kiss. She said,
Sardonic: "You had better blow your horn."
He smiled, strode out, and blew it. They assembled,
The eleven others, armed for adventure,
Hearing, as they went, with Joshua leading,
Words Moses had spoken: *See the people*
That dwell therein, whether they be strong or weak,
Few or many. And what cities they dwell in—
Whether in tents or in strongholds. Search the land
From the wilderness of Zin unto Rehob.
You will come, so says the Lord, to Hebron,
Where Ahiman, Sheshnai and Tamlai dwell,
The powerful children of Anak. Be of good courage . . .
So time passed and the spies did not return,
But the men of Israel said: "It is always the same.
He starts something off, and then we wait."
The women: "Like laying dishes for a meal
When you know there is nothing to eat." And the men,
        impatient:
"Is anything being *done?* Magic, that is.
Spells, anything, to get something *done?*"
But other men said: "That is against the law."
What was against the law appealed to Dathan,
Who lighted a fire and seasoned it with niter
And addressed the colored flames: "Tell us, we beg you,
O spirits of the desert, when these twelve
Are going to return." There was no reply.
"What do they say?" asked the credulous. Dathan said:

"They say they do not know."—"Try something else."
Dathan threw charcoal, sulphur mixed with niter
And raised a flashing spurt. "They say," he said,
"Never." But over mountain slopes in sunlight,
Under stars, standing on hilltops, seeing
Distant night fires, and soon—ah, blessed—hearing
Tumbling burns hurtling down rocks, dauntles the twelve
Fared on. One day, from behind bushes, some saw
Huge-limbed laughing men, bathing in a spring,
Speaking strange language, laving metal muscles,
Tough of sinew. Ahiman? Sheshnai? Tamlai?
If so, God help the Israelites, muttered Joshua.
While, back there in the encampment, the Israelites,
Mercifully shut off from future troubles,
Pondered present agonies, as they called them.
Dathan said: "Manna, nothing but manna. How about some
Flesh to eat, as in the old days?" chewing his manna
With a sour face, and his wife said: "Kill a sheep—"
"A priest has to do that for you," Dathan said.
"And no priest will do it. We have to, *he* says, *he*,
Conserve the livestock. God help us, or somebody."
His wife dreamed, looking into their fire, of Egypt:
"Remember the fish we used to eat, and the melons,
The leeks, cucumbers, onions, garlic?"—"Don't," he cried.
"You make me thirsty. Not till tomorrow midday
Does he strike the rock, his twice-weekly miracle."
No miracles in Eshcol, or all miracle,
The crystal plashing down, the pomegranates,
The grape clusters heavy on the vine,
While the spies stared incredulous before
Their thirst and hunger growled at idle fingers,
And then the fingers tore, cluster after cluster,
And the noon was a riot of juice. Juice-stained, they heard
What greatly qualified this juicy heaven,
Mouths open, dripping juice, listening to
An undoubted war chant. Some, from hill slopes, saw
A distant dust of an army, armor and swords
Catching the light, heard drums and horns and shouts,
And looked at each other, dismayed. *Be of good courage,*

So he had said. Much good would good courage do them,
Strong-limbed armies barring the way of Canaan
Of a people weak and weaponless, a people now
Cursing Moses: *Worker of miracles, work*
A proper miracle, give us proper food,
Or at least let us slaughter some of the sheep and kine
That we may fill our bellies with meat. He cried:
"Is there no end to your complaining?
Is not the Lord God looking after your needs?
Have I not told you till my very teeth
Are shaped like the letters of the words, that we are here
But for a space? The antechamber of your inheritance,
I call it that, and soon the doors will open
On Canaan, where you will feed fully of its richness,
Be clothed in suet like the kidney of the ox.
I warn you now—if any of you shall seek
To eat flesh meat against my will and the will
Of the Lord your God, it shall be accounted a curse."
And then the lifting of rocks and pebbles began,
The regular stoning of Moses who, angrily,
Shouted: "Fools, can you not understand?
We have no Egyptian gold or silver now.
We have only our flocks and cattle—the wealth
We take with us to Canaan. If we start killing—
Even a ram, even a bullock—all too soon
We shall have nothing." But still they hurled their stones
Till the troops hit back, and then they hurled only curses.
That evening, in proper furtiveness, a ewe was slain,
Some said by Dathan: Dathan was certainly one
Of the greasy tearers and munchers about a fire
Spitting with fat in the small hours. When arrest was made,
It was Dathan who smiled: "Very well, do your worst.
At least our bellies sing and roll with meat.
Would you gentlemen of the law care for a kidney
Or a hunk of haunch?" Moses, sitting in judgment,
Sighed, said: "I believe that some of you
Would eat your own mothers." Dawn was coming up.
"Meat meat—is there no other thought in your heads?
The gravity of the crime must be matched by—O Lord help me

Must I go down in their annals as the hard man,
Moses the cruel?" Dawn mounted higher. He heard,
Or thought he heard, jubilant noise from the sun,
And then he turned and, striding through the dew,
Twelve men seemed to be singing. Aaron said:
"The punishment—what is the punishment?"
And Moses said: "Not now, Aaron. Let us not talk of
Punishments now. See, they return, all twelve,
Singing and bearing poles, and on those poles—"
Soon they could see jostling pomegranates,
Figs ready to burst with sweetness, grapes,
All tied with vine ropes to poles borne on shoulders,
The poles sagging midway with the weight,
And the cheerful faces of the spies. "You see," Moses said
To his people, whose eyes were eating the promise
Of sugared juice in the distance, "that land, as we were told,
Is flowing with milk and honey, at least with fruit,
You wretched grumbling ingrates." Some ran out,
Not listening, to greet the approaching twelve, cheering,
And soon they were approaching with them, munching,
Dripping with juice. It was Shammua spoke first:
"We entered the land, Moses, as you instructed,
And it bursts with richness. These grapes and figs and
        pomegranates
We gathered by a brook that we call Eshcol—"
"Well-named, Eshcol," Moses smiled. "A grape cluster.
So we have planted at least one name of our own
In the land of Canaan. See, you foolish children,
The wealth of that land. And that land is ours—"
"The land is not ours," Shammua said. "We saw the people.
They dwell in walled cities and are warlike—"
"Giants," Shaphat said, "the children of Anak.
We saw them. Hittites, Jebusites—who were the others?"
Igal said: "Amorites, the mountain people.
And by the sea the Canaanites. It is not ours,
That land. We could not possibly prevail—"
"True," Shaphat said. "We have not the numbers.
We have not the weapons." Caleb spoke up at last
To cry that this was foolish and feeble talk.

"We are strong enough. We can strike now. *Must* strike now."
Moses turned to Joshua: "What do *you* say?"
And Joshua said: "I am of Caleb's mind.
We can do it. We have certain advantages.
They do not know our numbers. We can strike from
      the mountains—"
"And what," asked Moses of the others, "say the rest of you?"
At once a protesting babble. "*There is no comparison*
As to strength we saw them on parade
Huge armies we lack the power we lack the training
The weapons. But Caleb cried aloud: "It is
Strength of purpose you lack." Shaphat said:
"Look, we have been through all that land, a land
That would swallow us as a toad swallows a gnat.
The sons of Anak are giants. Compared to them,
We are as grasshoppers are to us." Then Dathan,
With whom Abiram stood, Abiram, a man
Who had suffered but said little, also Koreh,
Koreh, that strong upholder of the law,
Spoke in no loud voice, not at first. He said:
"Listen to me, Moses. We have borne much trouble
With hardly a murmur." Moses smiled at that.
"We were given a promise, and that was that we were to
Walk into this land of yours—without trouble,
For have we not had enough and more than enough
Of that? I say this now to you and think I say it
On the behalf of all: I would to God
We had died in the land of Egypt. I would to God
We had died in the wilderness. Why, tell us why
We have been brought towards this land to fall by the sword,
To see our wives and children cut to pieces.
What strange plan does this God of yours have in mind?"
Abiram spoke. "I vote we choose a new captain—
One who will better consult the people's interests—
One who will lead us back to Egypt." And he
Looked at Dathan, who looked modestly
Down at the ground. Moses spoke now to Koreh:
"You, sir, were the rigorous upholder
Of God's law. Do you then join this new party?"

Koreh, embarrassed, said: "I have to confess that—
Well, my confidence in your leadership (with respect)
Has long been wavering. I am of the people,
For the people. The people with me must come first,
And if the law turns sour and if the people
Cease to see good where no good is to be seen,
Then am I not right to waver? There is a feeling
That we ought to return to Egypt." Moses said:
"Never waver, Koreh. Ever be firm
For one thing or another. Never waver."
But now, spilling grape pips, fig sap, many mouths
Began to cry scorn for Moses; and for Abiram,
Dathan, Koreh, strong sounds of support.
Till Joshua cried: "Listen." But they would not.
So he took his horn from his side and blasted loud
And, taken by surprise, they listened. He said:
"The land we passed through—it is a good land.
It is *our* land. If the Lord delight in us,
He will bring us to that land. He will give it to us,
Against the opposition of mere giants."
Moses looking toward his own tribe of the Levites,
Saying: "The sons of Levi have no word
Either against or for me." Indeed they stood
With blank sad faces. shut mouths. "Decide," he said.
"At least *decide*." But they stood there, gnawing their lips.
"Milk and honey," sneered Abiram. It was taken as a sign
For the throwing of stones. Joshua cried again:
"I say this—do not rebel against the Lord.
Do not fear the peoples of that land.
We can chew them up like bread, for our teeth will be
The Lord's teeth. Their defense will melt like
Honey in the sun. The Lord is with us, not them.
Do not be afraid. Follow me. Fight."
So they threw and threw, there being plenty of stones.
And then a sharp-sided flint caught the brow of Moses
And he cursed the people, or tried to: "God's curse
On you who curse the Lord." He was struck again
And this time fell, though at once found himself standing
In a crystal desert, looking at a tabernacle

That was twenty suns, unflinching, hearing a voice:
"How long will this people provoke me?
How long will it be ere they believe me,
For all the signs which I have shown among them?
Because all those men which have seen my glory
And my miracles, which I did in Egypt and in the wilderness,
And have tempted me now these ten times,
And have not harkened to my voice,
Surely they shall not see the land which I
Promised unto their fathers.
Their carcasses shall fall in the wilderness.
They shall wander many years in the wilderness.
None now living shall come into that land,
Save Caleb the son of Jephunneh
And Joshua the son of Nun. But your little ones—
Them will I bring in, them,
And they shall know the land which ye have despised."
So Moses in the spirit stood erect.
But in the body lay stricken on his pallet,
While Zipporah wept and tended his wounds. Without,
In the place of assembly, Abiram spoke to many:
"He is about to die. I have this, friends,
On the best authority. He is only a mortal man.
You have now the choice of living or dying yourselves.
Who will lead you to life, if it is life you choose?
Egypt is far. Beyond those mountains there
There is hope that is near—food, water, life.
We do not seek a kingdom. We seek a place
Where we can enter quietly, live in peace—
In slavery, if need be. Slavery—
Is slavery worse than this life-in-death?" Doubtful,
Divided, the people knew not which way to turn.
Dathan had counseled Egypt, so had Abiram:
Now they tugged different ways: a choice of enslavements.
But when Moses, weak but beyond fear of dying,
Lay awake in his tent, Aaron came in to say
That now they had various kinds of revolt on their hands.
Some had gone over the mountains. Moses rose,
Helped by his brother, to look afar and saw them,

A band of climbing Israelites. He wept and raged,
Though feeble: "The Lord is not with them.
The enemy will see them—the Amalekites,
The Canaanites. Ah, the fools. The foolish children . . ."
By the Ark of the Covenant, Levites, some with packs,
Already ripe to move, still strove in
Justification of their timid revolt:
We are of the tribe of Moses, brothers, yes—
But are we not also the chosen of God?
Is it not of God himself we must seek counsel?
At least we find that God does not speak against us.
Has perhaps the Lord God forsaken Moses?
In Canaan, Ahiman and Sheshnai looked,
From the stream where they were bathing, up in wonder
At a strange horde, unarmed, on the mountaintop,
With sheep and goats in plenty. They ran in glee
And wetness the sun drank to speak of it.
To summon the drums and trumpets. And all too soon
The fugitives looked down, panic dawning,
Ripening, to see a dusty army flashing,
And many began to scramble back ready to curse,
When they had breath, the plan of Abiram.
Some held out longer, then fled, having seen things
They later were to unlade in front of Joshua:
Cut to pieces. My own father. They started
With chopping off his ring finger. They could not
Get the ring off so they. Horror, sobbing.
They are coming. They're getting their army together.
The Israelite camp filled with weeping, cursing,
The fluttering of fowls at the scent of the fox.
Joshua blew his horn, brought order, order,
Order of a sort. "Let no more try to leave.
You are all under my orders." At least forewarned,
Seeing in no surprise the flash of weapons
Coming over the mountain, the army, such as it was,
Had time to arm and assemble under Joshua.
A small armed guard, under the command of Aaron,
Guarded the tabernacle, rich gold in sunlight,
The enemy's, without a doubt, prime target.

So down they came, yelling, with drum thump,
With bray of horn, in dust stabbed with points of silver,
To the Israelite plain. The women screamed and scattered
While Joshua raised his spear. In the first skirmish,
The enemy was surprised—these were, then, after all,
No enfeebled people sucking goat teats. Joshua smote
Hard and hard. Caleb killed a giant.
But the enemy drove in to the center, seeing gold.
Aaron was pierced in the thigh, but the inner guard
Fought the more for his scream, beating them off,
The dirty defiling fingers. Within his tent,
Moses prayed, tried to rise, was held down
By Zipporah and Gershom, so prayed again:
They may not prevail. You, O Lord God,
May not suffer them to prevail. And the earth shook,
But it may have been a natural fault in the earth,
Or the shaking of the armies. He heard a trumpet
Crying retreat. Joshua, wiping sweat away, saw it—
Retreat. But it was the retreat of an army
That had had enough for the day, driving before it
Herds and cattle, also women. (They would return:
Rich fields for reaping here.) Among the women
Was the wife of Dathan, but Dathan did not weep,
Rather blew his rage to a white fire.

14 | THE DEATH OF DATHAN

THERE were three of them then, all in a sort of accord
Hammered out of necessity, as they saw it,
And, adorned like men of position, with men behind them,
They marched on Moses and Aaron. Moses, weak still,
Lay pale on his bed, seeing three princes approach—
Abiram, Koreh and, ahead of them, Dathan.
Dathan's rage was in check. "If I may speak—"
"You do not look like a man who seeks permission,"
Moses said. "Speak by all means, Dathan."
So Dathan spoke. "What I say I say
On behalf of my peers. What I say
I do not lightly say. What I say I say
After grave and long consideration—"
"And," said Aaron, "what is it that you say?"
Dathan said: "This. That we have reached the limit
Of endurance of your tyranny over us,
Prince Moses. You made promise of milk and honey
And silver and gold and a land over which our people,
The children of Israel, should rule." Moses said:
"The milk and honey were certainly promised, Dathan—"
"And what," said Dathan, "have we been given instead?
Starvation in the wilderness, death in the wilderness."
Moses said: "You, Dathan, have avoided
Both starvation and death with exemplary cunning.
Now will you come to your point?" And Dathan said:
"My point is that your day of rule is over—
Or soon will be. We have support in all the tribes."

Moses said: "I see. And what then do the
Usurping princes seek to do with their power?
Koreh is one of them, I see. At least he is no longer
Wavering." Dathan cried out. "You have failed,
Moses, failed, and you know you have failed.
The whole expedition has been a failure.
With your tricks and talk of an all-powerful God
You've swollen yourself to an imitation Pharaoh,
Forcing your failure upon us." Moses sighed
"You forget much, Dathan. You forget that I
Was once a prince of Egypt, laden with gems,
Stuffed with sweetmeats, suffocated with the
Perfume of courtesans. This is a strange power
I have taken on, is it not?—The burden of rule
Without its comforts: my palace a tent, my kingdom
A wilderness. I ask again: What is your policy,
Prince Dathan?" And Dathan replied: "To lead the tribes
Back to Egypt, but not into slavery.
To make, out of a sufficiency of power,
A treaty with the Pharaoh. To demand
That the God of the Israelites be of equal status
With any of the gods of Egypt." Aaron smiled
Frostily: "At least at last you believe in a
Sort of God of the Israelites. It is a beginning—"
"A true beginning," Dathan said, "will be to
Show your impotence by wresting this thing away—
This ark you use for holding the people down.
We can provide our own priests—" Aaron said:
"For holding the people down." And Moses: "Dathan,
Dathan—I confess my failure as a teacher.
It seems I have taught you nothing. God chooses man.
Man does not choose God. God shows how he chooses
Through signs—signs. What signs do you have?"
Dathan said: "If by signs you mean trickery—"
And Moses: "I see you all carry your rods
Of potential rule. Those are a kind of sign—"
"Those sticks," said Dathan, "stand for the confidence
Of the twelve tribes in our mission," raising his.
"We are delegated to speak for them all." Moses said:

"Aaron, cast your rod to the ground." He did so.
"Now, let the rest of you contend
With the priestly power of Aaron. Signs, signs—
What have we, any of us, but signs?" Then Dathan:
"More Egyptian trickery. Foolishness.
An old man's foolishness." Moses said to him:
"Indulge an old man's foolishness a while.
You will not have to suffer it much longer."
So Dathan, sneering, cast his rod down, and the others,
Abiram and Koreh, cast down theirs.
"What will you do with Aaron's?" Dathan grinned.
"Turn it into a serpent? That's an old trick."
But as he spoke he ceased to smirk: the rod
Of Aaron put out leaves and flowers and fruit.
The others stayed but rods. Then Moses said,
Wearily: "I have warned you often enough
In my time, Dathan, and now I swear to you
That this warning shall be final. Hear me, then.
Seek not to rise against the Lord your God.
To you all I say this—bear back my word to the others.
Tempt not the Lord your God, lest the ground
Open under your feet and swallow you."
But Dathan and his fellows strode away,
With no further word, while Aaron
Picked up his rod, smelt at a budding rose,
Saw the rose fade, the fruit wrinkle, the leaves
Drop, become nothing before they reached the earth.
That night, in torchlight, Moses spoke to his people:
"Keep, I warn you, away from the tents of the wicked.
Touch, I warn you, nothing of theirs, lest ye
Be consumed in all their sins. Pay heed to my words.
You shall now know, once for all, that the Lord chooses,
That men do not. And if these men—pay heed—
Die the common death of all men,
Be visited after the visitation
Of all men, then the Lord has not sent me.
But if the Lord your God makes a new thing,
And the earth opens her mouth and swallows them
And they go down swiftly to the pit—then, pay heed,

You shall understand these men have provoked the Lord."
But Dathan, Abiram, Koreh blasphemously
Attired themselves like priests, scoffing at his words,
And they stood before the tabernacle like priests,
And Dathan spoke out strong: "So. We stand here
By the tabernacle to tell you that your God,
The God of the people, speaks through the people
By means of the voice of them that the people have chosen,
That what the people have chosen as prudent and wise
Will be confirmed by the God of the people. We,
The people, choose to return to Egypt, there
To live in peace and fatness. Will our God
Say nay?" And that word was caught up: *nay* and *nay*
In the torchlight. So Moses shut his eyes
That he might not see what he knew must follow,
Hearing only thunder, the jolting of the earth,
Cries of terror, opening his eyes to see
What he knew he must see: dust and enveloping smoke
About the tabernacle, and the three false priests
Not there, but the people on their knees in terror.
Dathan no more: the earth had eaten Dathan.
And Moses spoke to himself: *Yet mercy is infinite.*
At least let us believe so. Dathan, Dathan,
I shall miss your thorn in my side . . .
Now, by a different way, skirting the mountains
And the fierce foes beyond them, in a new unity,
But wretched, they fared on, leaving behind
Carcasses in the desert, as foretold,
Seeking Mount Hor. Jolted in a cart,
Attended by wife and sons, Aaron lay,
The wound in his thigh grown green, in great pain,
With nauseous ointments lapped by the blowflies. "So,"
Eliseba his wife said, "your reward
For protecting that tabernacle of yours." She wept.
"The pain," he said, "grows less. The wound will sleep—"
"But not the fever. The fever is much awake."
Aaron said: "I will be better at the oasis.
Trees and running water. Fruit." She wiped his lips
With a towel, and he spoke to Eleazar,

His son, saying: "You know what you must do
When we reach Mount Hor?" And the son replied:
"I must become a priest."—"A priest," said his father.
"You must take over my office, wear my garments.
Eleazar the priest. Your mother will be proud."
But she said: "Do not talk like that." And Aaron:
"It is never too soon to prepare him for the task.
It is the task and the glory that his sons
And his sons' sons must fulfill till the end of our race.
A task and a glory he will take with him into Canaan.
It is he who will perform the rite of thanksgiving."
But Eliseba said: "You will be well soon.
You will be there in all your robes and glory."
But Aaron replied: "The journey is by no means over.
We cannot enter in peace. Bitter enemies—
Those are to be faced. Oasis to oasis,
Skirting the promised land, seeking a way in
That is not to be granted so easily. Eliseba,
You have known a hard life."—"All life is hard,"
She said. "It is the nature of life
To be hard. But there have been— Well, shall I say
The hardness has made the pleasures more pleasurable.
I do not complain. Try now to sleep a little."
So she laid his head in her bosom, and he slept.
But slept less, raving, as the fever raved,
And ceased to rave when they came in sight of the mountain,
Speaking strange words softly, and soon no words,
No breath for words. She shut his eyes forever.
He was borne on a litter, in his priestly robes,
Up to the mountaintop. Gently, Moses
Took off the priestly garments and invested
Eleazar, the son of Aaron, in them,
And Eleazar led the chant, against the morning,
Blessing all, finally blessing his father
Who lay in the morning forever. Moses spoke:
"I speak of him as my brother first—faithful,
Unwavering in his faith. My very voice,
My other heart. And of the house of Israel
None was more brave, more steadfast. His mouth was of gold,

The spirit of the Lord burned in him. Now we see him
Gathered to his fathers. God grant him rest.
God grant that his spirit ever animate
The race he so adorned, lending it
Something of his strength, of his faith.
So be it." But to himself he said:
And how long will the race last? We are dying,
The old men are dying. Can the young
Survive? Can they keep the fire alight? He foresaw
A desert of corpses, foreheard traveling voices:
Dead so long ago. So much time passed.
That body there—that could be my father's.
A powerful people—at least a numerous people.
Have they disappeared? Are they gone forever?
The end of them, the end of them, I'd say.
It would be a kind act to bury these dead.
But they are already buried. Already forgotten.
Just dead bodies. Without a name.
Without a race. He shook the voices away,
And turned again to the task of quietening
Real voices, living voices. So they moved towards Edom,
Living bodies, with a name, with a race, moved.
And one day, in the palace of the king of Edom,
A crude barbaric throneroom, eating grapes,
While a chamberlain spoke. "*Ganas voti,*" the king said.
So in they came, dusty, travel-worn, bowing,
Joshua and Caleb: "May we speak, sir king?"
The king nodded, spitting grape seeds. Joshua:
"You will have heard of our nation. Israel.
We have been in bondage to Egypt for many years,
Not only our generation but generations
And generations before us. We cried out to the Lord
And the Lord brought us forth out of Egypt. Now we are in
Kadesh, on the border of your kingdom.
We are sent to ask leave to pass
Peacefully through your country." The chamberlain
Translated into the dialect of the kingdom:
The king showed little interest. Caleb said:
"We promise, majesty, not to pass through your fields,

Or through your vineyards. We promise not to drink
Of the waters of your wells. We promise to go
Only by the king's highway—yours, majesty.
We will not turn to the right hand nor to the left,
Until we have passed your borders." The king listened,
Splitting a fig now, and at length said: "*Nor vah.*"
"I am instructed," said the chamberlain, "to inform you
That the answer is no." The king spoke a longer sentence:
"*Go nadi daya, goro mi nadi nadi in vebu—*"
"His majesty's words are these: if you try to pass,
We will slay you all with the sword." Regretfully.
"That was sufficiently plain," Joshua said.
"I am instructed to add that if our people
Or their cattle drink of the water of your kingdom,
Then we will pay for it." The king waved a violent fig:
"*Garata karvol. Nor vah nor vah.*" The chamberlain
Began to translate, but Joshua wearily said:
"We understand." They looked at each other wearily.
The king offered grapes, figs. They refused.
Handmaidens. Regretfully, they refused.
So Moses sought another road, young men about him,
Men even younger than Caleb and Joshua,
While he traced a map in the sand, saying: "Yes,
We are ready to *progress*, Joshua." They smiled.
"But not by the northern road. We are, thank God,
Much better warriors than we were, but hardly
Good enough yet to face those northern armies.
So we have to think of another road." But all roads
Led, it seemed, to war—skirmishes
With dirty desert people, formal battles
With men in armor, their trumpets sweet and polished,
Encounters with barbarous hosts that spoke a language
Of growls and coughs. But, as time passed, the Israelite banners
Prevailed more. A matter of training. Stolen arms.
Even a matter of silver trumpets. There was a night
When the Israelite warriors, proud of being warriors,
Feasted and listened, full, to a blind harpist
Who sang of their strength: "Woe to thee, Moab.
Thou art undone, O people of Chemosh.

We have shot at them. Heshbon is perished
Even unto Dibon. And we have laid them
Waste even unto Nophah." Caleb, wine-flushed, said:
"And yet there was a time, not long ago,
When we couldn't win a single battle." Joshua,
Wine-flushed, said: "Discipline. Generalship.
Youth. New methods." The blind band sang:

> And we turned and went up by the way of Bashan.
> And Og the king of Bashan went out against us.
> He and all his people, to the battle at Edrei.
> And the Lord said unto Moses: Fear him not,
> And thou shalt do unto him as thou didst
> Unto Sihon, king of the Amorites.
> So we smote them and his sons and all his people.
> Until, halleluiah, none was left alive,
> And we possessed his land.

Warriors listening,
Scarred, patched, amputated, reminiscent,
Not above tears, cheering the end of the song.
"Discipline," Joshua said. "Generalship.
And God, of course. God is on our side."
Wine-flushed, scarred, tough in the flare of the fires.

15 | BALAAM

Woe to thee, Moab. That was a proleptic phrase.
They were hearing, in Moab, of a tough, scarred people,
Young, with a leader so aged as to be mythical
And hence unaging. In the royal palace at Moab
The King, Balak, listened to a minister saying,
In loud agitation to another minister;
"Have I ever denied it? I said all along
They were, are, a dangerous people." The king said:
"Where are they now?" The second minister pointed
To a crude map on sheepskin: "There. You see.
This side of Jericho. By Jordan river.
They have set up their tents on the plains of Moab."
So the king cried: "My territory. Do you mark that?"
And the first minister: "As I said before,
They were, are, a dangerous people. Also they are
A *breeding* people. Babies scarce out of the cradle
Doing arms drill, or so we are told. And look what they did
To the Amorites." The king said: "What did they
Do to the Amorites?" The second minister said:
"Your majesty was presented with a comprehensive report."
King Balak said: "Yes yes, mass castration or something.
I know." And the first: "With respect, your majesty.
Slaughter, yes. But no atrocities. They are not a
Castrating people." The king said: "Slaughter is enough.
As the ox licks up the grass of the meadow. Eh?
Eh?" An apt simile, they all agreed.
"How many men can we put in the field?" said the king.

"Not enough," he was told. "It's a matter of numbers,
Not of courage or organization. No,
Certainly by no manner of means enough."
King Balak thought and at length said: "How about a curse?"
A curse, sir? "A curse, a malediction. Scare them off.
A religious people, are they? Very well,
They will know all about curses. Potent weapons.
Also economical. A curse." The second minister
Smiled wanly and said: "Ah, Balaam. Balaam—"
"Balaam, Balaam, a very powerful blesser
And an equally powerful, if not more so, curser.
Where is Balaam these days?" The ministers knew.
"In Pethor, your majesty. You know—by the river."
Balaam was fishing happily in the river,
Singing a song of his youth. As he grew older
His youth grew clearer. A song of his childhood.
A fat short man, amiable, a powerful curser,
This being his profession. Fishing in the sun,
He scowled when he saw a shadow come over him
And yet the sun still there. Looking up,
He saw that the shadow was of four men, gentlemen,
Of high rank certainly, standing there. He said:
"Ah, gentlemen. You I know, I think.
I am afraid the other gentlemen—" Two elders from Moab:
These he knew. The others? "Greetings, Balaam,"
Said one of the Moabites. "We are come from the king.
These gentlemen are from Midian. We bear you word
From the court of Moab. The gentlemen of Midian
Wish to be associated with our mission."
Balaam said: "Ah, come, come then, got you,"
Landing a carp. Then: "Mission? Message?" A fine one.
The elder Moabite read aloud from a tablet:
"Behold, there is a people come out of Egypt.
Behold, this people covers the face of the earth
And abides over against me. Come now, I pray you, therefore
Curse me this people, for they are too mighty for me.
Then perhaps I shall prevail, drive them out of the land.
For I know well that he whom you bless is blessed,
And he whom you curse is cursed." Balaam heard that,

Complacent, then he said: "The king's own words?"
The elder said: "You will recognize the style."
Balaam rose and said: "Lodge here tonight.
Plenty of fish, as you see. I have to consult—
I must— You understand there are certain things
I shall have to do." They understood. "And in the morning
I hope you may take back word to— How is his majesty?"
Distressed, they said. Very fine carp, they said.
They ate them all that night, sucking the bones,
And drank the thick black wine of Pethor. Balaam,
Expansive, told tales of cursings. "Ah, yes, gentlemen.
That was one of my better curses. It was
Extremely efficacious." The eldest Moabite:
"I hope you can provide an even better one.
One worthy of this accursed people."—"Accursed?"
One of the Midianites said. "That is surely
A little premature." They laughed, finished the wine,
And Balaam said: "Now, I will go to my sanctum
And brew up my curse. Excuse me, gentlemen."
In what he called his sanctum, reeking of mold,
Fish glue, asafetida, by a fish-oil lamp
He muttered over signs on old sheepskin, a skull,
A dried crocodile for company. Then the skull spoke.
Out of the sempiternal grin of the skull—
Or was it the crocodile's?—words came,
Gentle enough: *Who are these men with you?*
Balaam gaped, gaped again, then answered:
"Balak, the son of Zippor, king of Moab,
Sent them to me. But who are you, who *are* you?"
The voice said: *With what word?* "Who are you?" gaped
Balaam. "Who?" *With what word?* Balaam took the
Tablet and read from it, shaking: "Behold,
There is a people come out of Egypt, which
Covers the face of the earth. Come now, curse me
Them, then perhaps I shall prevail—" The voice said:
Listen, Balaam. You shall not curse this people.
For the Lord has already blessed them. You hear, Balaam?
"Lord Lord what is this Lord?" *The Lord God,*
Balaam. "But I have an instruction, an order—

From the king himself. What is this *Lord God?*"
The voice said, quietly still: *I am the king*
Of your king and all kings that ever were
And shall be. Therefore, Balaam, I say to you:
You shall not go forth to curse the children of Israel.
So the skull or crocodile was silent. Balaam sat,
Gaping. A dream? No, not a dream. Nor wine,
Not wine, he knew the effects of wine.
The emissaries snored. He sat there, gaping.
In the morning, at first light, as they smacked dry mouths,
Squinting for the wine jug, he told them, spluttered,
Saying: "You understand? You understand me?
It was the voice of the *Lord God*, so he is called—"
"And not," said an elder, ringing the taste of the wine
On his morning mouth, "some devil of your own conjuring?
Some devil that consults your interests? I'm empowered to say,
On the king's behalf that he had thought of some
Highly tangible reward." But Balaam cried:
"If Balak should give me his palace crammed with silver,
Gold too, rubies, I could not go
Beyond the word of this Lord God, as he is called.
"And if Balak should, say, order decapitation,
Preceded by certain ingenuities
Of torture?" Balaam stoutly said: "This Lord God
Would intervene, of this I am sure." The second elder,
Not much of a talker, spoke, rasping, saying:
"Why not call on him now for assurance, Balaam?
Are you certain, by the way, that he exists?
That he was not a phantom induced by carp flesh
And the damnably heavy wine of Pethor?" Balaam,
Distressed, said nothing. And the first elder smiled:
"Come then, O Balaam of my heart, let us go.
There is work to be done, if cursing
Can properly be called work." Balaam gulped, saying:
"Where do I have to go?" The elders told him:
"To the plains of Moab, the tents of the Israelites—
There to do your cursing. You have cursing to do."
The road they took, Balaam ahead on his ass,
Led to a narrow way between two vineyards.

Balaam with servants behind, behind four elders,
Riding an ass, which he preferred to a horse,
Being easier, for one of his bulk, to mount,
Found that the ass responded with a bray of fear
To something she saw, something he did not see.
And she tried to get from the way of what she saw,
Thrusting towards one of the walls. He whipped her, while
The emissaries behind expressed impatience, anxious
To get the cursing over. So she took the road
Again and again brayed fear, thrusting towards the
Other wall. Balaam yelled and beat her,
But, taking the path again, this time she fell
And Balaam fell with her. He rose, his anger was great,
He whipped and whipped, panting. And now she spoke.
Now she spoke. She brayed: "What have I done to you?
Why must you beat me three times?" Balaam cried:
"Who said that? Who spoke then? Was it you?
You? If I had a sword I'd thrust it straight
Into your faithless flank." So the ass brayed:
"Kill me? Faithless? Am I not your beast?
Have you not ridden me every day?" He said,
Panting: "You mocked me. Do you hear? You mocked me."
And the ass said: "Did I ever mock you before?"
Balaam wept (he is drunk, he is old, he is mad,
The emissaries said to each other). "No."
And he turned to them and to his servants. "Did this
Animal really speak? Am I going mad?"
An elder from Midian spoke. "A touch of the sun."
And on that word light brighter than sunlight struck
Balaam, him only, and he fell flat on his face,
Hearing the voice of last night out of the sky:
Your beast saw me and turned thrice from the path.
The Lord God is no figment of man's mind
But very reality which even the beasts may know.
Your ass has saved you by turning you from the path.
For, Balaam, if you had ridden into my path,
Then surely I would have slain you. Balaam sobbed,
Raised his terrified head towards the light,
Then lowered it, blinded. "I have sinned, O Lord.

I have displeased you. I will go back again."
No, said the voice. *Go to the court of the king*
And speak there what I shall put in your mouth to speak.
Then the great light faded, leaving the little light,
Birds singing, the ass cropping vine leaves,
And Balaam said, trembling: "We must go to the king."
The eldest elder nodded, saying: "Yes.
The king must see you. You are obviously
In no fit state for cursing." So, in the palace of Moab,
The king was loud: "Why? *Why?* You had your orders.
Your orders were clear. You were to put a curse
On the hosts of Israel. And now you come babbling
About the *Lord God*, whoever he is
Are you now in the pay of the Israelites?
Have they cast a spell on you? Are even their
Magicians more potent than ours?" But Balaam said:
"I have no power to curse the Israelites.
All I may speak is what the Lord God
Puts in my mouth to speak." The king cried: "God?
God? You mean the god of the Israelites?"
Balaam said, humbly enough: "It seems to me
That such language is foolish. I speak with respect.
No, I do not. Respect and disrespect
To kings and men in high places—what do they mean
To me now? It seems to me that there is only
One God, and though the Israelites
May have found this out before other men, yet this
Does not make him merely a God of the Israelites.
But certainly this God will not curse the Israelites."
King Balak cried: "We have a god of our own.
It seems to me that you have wronged our god.
Ba'al has turned against you. Reparation,
Sacrifice is called for." But Balaam shook his head,
Saying: "There is only one God,
So this Lord God said to me. And idolatry
Is an abomination before the Lord."
He seemed ready then to fall into a trance.
The court was shocked at his blasphemy, the king
Outraged. When night fell, before the idol Ba'al,

With flares and aromatic gums burning, priests
Dispatching a ram with knives, then firing the flesh
On the altar, an abomination before the Lord,
Balaam was dragged, under guard, forcibly enrobed
And ordered by the king himself to curse, but he could not.
Now, Balaam. Beg of our god what I beg of you.
A curse on the Israelites. But he could not.
Instead he spoke, as it seemed, for some not present:
"Balak the king has brought me to this high place
Before the idol Ba'al. And he has said:
Come, curse Israel, curse the blood of Jacob.
But how shall I curse whom God has not cursed? How
Defy whom the Lord has not defied? From the top
Of the rocks I see him, and from the hills
I behold him. Let me die the death of the righteous
Before I curse Israel and the God of Israel."
The king wept aloud: "What have you done to me?
I took you to curse my enemies: behold, you bless them."
And Balaam said: "The Lord God is not a man,
That he should lie, neither the son of man,
That he should repent. Has he said, and shall he not do it?
Has he spoken and shall he not make it good?
Behold, I have received commandment to bless and I cannot
Reverse it." At the king's sign he was led away,
Crying out: "God brought them out of Egypt.
His strength is the strength of the unicorn. Behold,
The people shall rise up as a great lion,
And lift themselves up as a young lion." They imprisoned him,
Manacled him to a wall, with serpents about,
Toads and scorpions, and thonged whips ready.
The king, troubled, said: "If you will not curse them,
Then at least do not bless them. Let us have you
Neutral in the fight that is to come."
But Balaam said: "I shall see him, though not now.
I shall behold him, but not nigh. There shall come
A star out of Jacob, and a scepter
Shall rise out of Israel and shall smite
The corners of Moab and all the children of Midian."
The king struck him in the face, twice, thrice,

But Balaam cried: "Moab shall be a possession,
And Israel shall do valiantly." The King, in disgust,
Said: "Loosen his chains. Let the madman go.
Send him out into the wilderness,
On that talking donkey of his." And they did so.
The Israelites in their tents woke at sunrise to hear
A voice raised to the sky, speaking their own tongue:
"How goodly are thy tents, O Jacob,
And thy tents, O Israel. As the valleys are they spread forth,
As gardens by the river's side, as the trees
Of lignaloes which the Lord has planted,
And as cedar trees beside the waters." Balaam
Had come riding ecstatic into their camp,
His ass placid beneath him. He cried aloud:
"He shall pour the water out of his buckets,
And his seed shall be in many waters,
And his king shall be higher than Agag,
And his kingdoms shall be exalted." The Israelites
Lined his path in wonder, and Balaam cried:
"God brought them forth out of Egypt. He has the strength
Of a unicorn. He shall eat up the nations his enemies,
And break their bones, and pierce them through with arrows."
Moses came from his tent to see and hear
This prodigy: a fat old man on an ass,
Declaiming to heaven: "He couched, he lay down as a lion,
And as a great lion. Who shall stir him up?
Blessed is he that blesses thee, and cursed
Is he that curses thee." Moses said:
"Whoever he is, he needs to be looked after."
So gently Balaam on his ass was led
Towards the tents of the high. "She spoke," he cried.
"She was fired with the fire of the Lord, and behold she spoke."
The ass was led to grass, and Balaam laid
Gently in Joshua's bed. They listened to him,
Joshua, Caleb, Eleazar, Moses,
With grave attention, while the younger children
Spoke to the ass, saying: "What is your name?
Where do you come from?" And the ass said nothing,
Finding the grass good. But Balaam cried:

"Behold, the great truth is come upon me.
He is a God of all things, halleluiah,
To one of the uncircumcised, a son of Moab,
He shone like a great light and so shines still.
Halleluiah. And the vessel of the Lord,
Which is Israel, shall prevail, and God shall prevail.
Halleluiah, halleluiah." Moses spoke to Joshua,
Quietly, half-fearful, half-unwilling to believe:
"So—the Lord God spreads his dominion.
Slowly. Almost cautiously. And the days of bloodshed
May soon be at an end. Our land may fall to us
Like a ripe pomegranate. Without a struggle.
Without the snipping of a single lock of hair
Or the bruising of a finger." But Joshua knew
He spoke too soon. Balaam cried on and on:
"Strong is the dwelling place of the most high.
Thou puttest thy nest in a rock. And ships shall come
From the coast of Chittim, and the enemies of the Lord
Shall perish forever and ever. Halleluiah."
And the ass without, raising her teeth from the grass,
Raised her voice and brayed. "It was *Amen*,"
The children said. "It sounded like *Amen*."

16 ZIMRI

So THAT, and they praised God for it, was all behind them:
The Dead Sea stretching in sunlight like a living one,
The boys diving into it for coolness
Shocked at not sinking, borne up by the hands
Of hidden water giants. They had shrieked, splashed,
Splashed, tasted. *Salt*, they had cried, *salt*.
Salt indeed, a salt lake set in a saltscape
Glooming with crystalline menace in the sun.
All we need is something to eat with it.
Salt salt salt. Remembering grandmothers' stories,
The women saying: "The wife of Lot must he here
Somewhere." and the men: "She could be anywhere."
Zipporah moaning: "Salt. Salt in my throat.
Soon surely we shall meet the fresh springs.
Why do we move so slowly, Gershom?" They were not
Moving at all: the tents had been set up
In the salt desert, salt under a salt moon.
But now the plain of Moab, with Moses saying:
"You think we can travel safely?" Joshua replying:
"We can never travel safely. The strength of Moab
Is still an unknown, and Moab has many friends.
Do not take Balaam as a sign of the weakening of Moab."
Moses smiled sadly: "Driven mad by the word of the Lord.
Poor Balaam." (Happy Balaam rode on his ass
Through the Israelite encampment, crying to the sky:
"For the Lord of the Israelites is all things.
Behold, he is in the creeping worm of the earth

And in the fiery lioness that is the sun.
He is unicorn and tiger and his name
Shall be blessed for ever and ever. Halleluiah."
And a sardonic Israelite: "*Halleluiah*.")
"Caution, then," said Moses. "We must send patrols
To learn about their defenses. And the general attitude
Of the Moabite population. We need them friendly.
We need their wells and pasturelands." Joshua said:
"But we must push on. Time is short." Then Moses:
"You were never a discreet man, Joshua. My time
Is certainly short, but do not remind me of it.
I shall see the Jordan before I die—fear not."
Joshua said: "I did not mean that. I meant
That the patience of our people can hardly be
Tried much longer. They are sick of wandering—"
"Oh, the young are patient enough. As for the old—
Well, there are few of us left. Aaron gone,
His poor wife Eliseba. And, soon, very soon—"
He sighed. "None is exempt, Joshua. The earth
Is hungry for us all. But that is what I meant
When I said we must stay here a little while.
I do not think she can very well be—moved."
Wasted with fever, Zipporah cried: "Tomorrow.
We shall see him tomorrow, then?" And Gershom:
"Who, mother?"—"My father, of course. And my sisters.
Those that are left. But not those wicked men
Who keep beating us away from the well. He took his stick
        to them.
He ran down the hill and trounced them and they ran off
        howling.
He was very strong in those days." And Gershom said:
"Is still. Is still very strong." (Very strong
In the synod, explaining the law at that very moment:
"The line must be drawn wide, very wide. It is the margin
That is the essence of the law. Thus, we condemn
The eating of the flesh of swine, and why?
It is not enough to say that it is unclean.
If you eat the flesh raw you will, as we know,
Contract disease: your belly will writhe with serpents.

If you eat it well-roasted you will be safe,
Since great heat kills the eggs of the serpents within
The body of the beast. Now who is to draw the line
Between well-roasted and ill-roasted? Who, indeed,
Is to draw the line between the roast and the raw?
It is safer to draw the margin too far out
And condemn the eating of swine's flesh altogether.
And so with marriage—always the safe margin.
Marry your brother's daughter; soon enough
Others will marry their mother's sisters, even
Their sisters, even their mothers. Draw the line
Far out, always far out, remember that.")
And Zipporah rambled more. "It will be pleasant
To sit by the well and talk. And sing. And play
Games with the ball as we used to. Waiting still
For the strong man from the strange land over the mountains
To come and fight the bad men by the well.
He will come with sunrise. Is it sunrise yet?"
Not waiting for an answer. "Sunrise. There is a
God in the sun, did you know that? And a god in the moon.
But the god of the sun is made out of fire. He has a
Beard of fire. And he eats fire." Then she cried out:
"Why do you give me fire to eat? Why do you
Keep pouring fire down my throat? Cold water—
From my father's well. Give me that, give it me."
Moses stood, sad, resigned: a matter of waiting.
He went out into the sunrise. Joshua said:
"The patrols are leaving now. It would be good
If you could give them a word of encouragement—"
"I cannot give her water from her father's well,"
Sighed Moses, "but I can always give encouragement."
The patrols were assembling now. Moses saw
A young man he thought he knew, one tall and clean
And upright. "Zimri," he said. "Zimri, is it not?"
The young man held himself stiff, answering: "Sir.
The son of Salu. Of the tribe of Simeon—"
"I knew your father," Moses said. "He was brave.
I trust his son takes after him." *Sir.* And then,
Raising his voice in the sunrise, Moses spoke

To the entire parade: "What you have to do
Is to find out what chance we have of passing
Through Moabite territory in safety. You may find
That the people are friendly. Do not be afraid
Of admitting you are Israelites. Watch out
Less for fights than for snares. The king or his princes
May arrange a feast and soak you in Moabite wine.
Then, while you are snoring, your throats may be quietly cut
See what amenities are available: wells, pasture.
Avoid their women. This is a pagan people.
They worship a false god. Do not be drawn in.
They practice all manner of abominations.
Do not be corrupted. Go, with my blessing."
Zimri, presenting the shining face of one
Who is incorruptible, said, firmly: "*Sir*."
And so they passed, in their several patrols, to Moab—
Gentle pasture, gentle people, pagan though,
Hence corruptive. Igal and Shaphat entered.
A pleasant town, seeing a marketplace
Where fruit and roots and sheep and goats were chaffered for,
Seeing a troupe of acrobats perform,
Seeing women, veiled but giggling,
Wagging provocative haunches. At an upper window
A lady sat in indolent enjoyment
Of the admiration of the street, fanned by a girl.
They sought and found a town office and, to a clerk,
In their own speech, slowly, said what their mission was.
They were understood and led to an inner room
Where an elegant officer sat but rose when they entered,
Offering cushions to sit upon, offering wine.
But they refused the wine, said who they were
And what they wished. "Yes. I understand you—"
"We naturally undertake to respect all property
As well as human life. We will certainly pay
For damage inadvertently done." And the officer:
"How will you pay?"—"In sheep. In cattle—"
"I see," he said. "Not in slaves? Or women?"
Igal said: "We do not sell our women.
And we do not keep slaves." Shaphat added to that:

"We have ourselves been enslaved—to the Egyptians.
Or so they tell us—it is rather a long time ago."
The officer said: "The story of your people
Has traveled even to our cities. So. Now I see
Real live Israelites in the flesh. Not very much flesh,
If I may say so." Igal said: "We are a lean folk.
That comes, I would say, of not living in cities."
And Shaphat: "A chosen people has to be
A lean people." The officer smiled. "But has also
To beg occasionally of the unchosen—and the fat—"
"Oh, we do not beg, sir," said Igal. "We merely request."
The officer said: "With an army behind you? I do not
Think we can very well refuse your request.
We like to think of ourselves as *hospitable*—"
"And the wells?" said Shaphat. "The grazing lands
        to the north?"
"You have, I hear, been living off salt," said the officer.
"It would not be *hospitable* to send you back to it.
Salt is good, but only in moderation."
And so the Israelites moved into the kingdom of Moab.
But Moses said to Joshua: "Towns. Towns.
Very corruptive places." Joshua said:
"We shall, we hope, be building towns ourselves."
But Moses shook his head: "Market towns perhaps,
Full of sheep dung. Call them disposable towns.
I am thinking rather of the cities where the citizens
Amass possessions—jewels and golden bedsteads.
Compromise, fatness, wavering in the faith.
Corruption. Even our short time here is dangerous.
The religion of Ba'al is seductive, Joshua.
We must watch our people." Caleb said: "We know that.
Zimri is watching. He has appointed himself
A kind of moral spy." And Moses said:
"A young man of good family. Reliable."
(Zimri walking watchfully in the evening,
Passing signs of corruption—laughing girls
Selling themselves for an hour or a night, swine flesh,
Drunken singing. He walked watchfully.)
"Oh yes," Caleb said. "Very reliable."

But Zipporah lingered at death's gate. In the night,
Moses spoke to his God: "Let her go in peace.
I shall have no power over her final agony.
Then, soon, there will be very few of us
Left over from the old days. And Joshua and Caleb—
They alone of the old days shall enter the land.
Not I, because of my sin of doubt. So be it.
But what then is left for me now? Let the day come soon,
For all things are ready—a people in good heart,
A people that learns to know its God. Let me see then
The river and the land from the high places,
And then be set free." He heard wailing
From the tent where Zipporah lay and bowed his head,
Though dry-eyed. *What then is left for me now?*
Zimri in daylight, walking the streets, observed
A public monument depicting men
Half-beast half-fish, engaged in contorted acts
Of love unknown to the Israelites. He saw
A woman, all brown blubber, laden with jewels,
Being carreid on a litter, on her lap
A silver sweet dish piled with powdery sweetmeats,
Powder and sugar about her mouth. Two flunkies
Whipped beggars and children out of her path. He saw
A blind man, in the final stage of some pox
Unknown to the Israelites, being led by a boy
In the first stage of some pox unknown to the Israelites.
He saw a vendor crying his works of art:
A frank act of sodomy in silver,
A man eating a cat alive, an image
Of Ba'al both foul and seductive, the rarest modes
Of love on wood or copper. And then he came
To an open-air feast, a table loaded heavy
With strange dishes. Beggars hungrily watched
But were beaten away by men with staves. Odd scraps
Of odd-looking meat were thrown at them: they gnawed
At bones like dogs. And Zimri, horrified, saw
Two Israelites at the feast, wearing the apparel
Of the Army of Israel. Their host, a gross Moabite
With a moon belly, urged them to eat and swill:

"Nothing like this in the wilderness, my boys—
Lobsters fresh from the coast—crack one, crunch one,
Sausages—try one, try several. And this dish
Is one of my cook's great prides: an unborn calf
Cooked in its mother's milk. Fall to. Eat, eat."
Zimri waited, collected a patrol,
And drove the drunken offenders, bellies taut,
Back to the camp and judgment. Joshua raged:
"Why not? I will tell you why not—because it is
Expressly forbidden by the food laws: that's why not.
Ten days on fatigues: you'll soon learn why not."
Zimri in night town, walking amid torches,
Music, dance, passed a man and a woman
Embracing naked and frankly in the shadows.
He shuddered, then grew angry when he observed
An Israelite he knew—Gaddiel, son of Sodi?
Mounting steps to a temple, or what seemed to be
A temple, its front carved with contorted bodies
In acts of love unknown to the Israelites.
He followed but had already lost him in the shadows
When he entered a chamber leading off the porch
            of the temple,
Lighted by torches and spitting oil lamps, gross
With pagan effigies. His heart thumped, he looked about him,
And then a woman emerged from the shadows, a Moabite,
In garments he took for those of a priestess, ugly,
Obscenely so, appallingly, seductively so.
She spoke honey: "You, sir, are a stranger—"
"An Israelite," he answered, his voice not
Well in control, and she said: "Ah, a follower
Of the new god we are hearing so much about.
The god of vengeance which is called justice." He:
"A God of love, we are taught. Of love. A God."
But she said, smiling: "So—not a new god, then.
You are interested, stranger, in our faith?"
Stiffly he said: "My own faith is enough
To keep my organ of faith fully occupied.
Other faiths are an abomination, so we are taught.
Many gods—all of them unclean:

The way of the Moabites, we are taught, much like
The way of the accursed Egyptians." She said:
"The Egyptian gods are gods of death—so *we* are taught."
He said: "Madam, you have been well instructed.
I must tell you that I am here officially.
Are Israelites frequenting this temple? I thought I saw
One enter now." She said: "Israelites, Moabites—
The names mean nothing. Servants of Ba'al
Come to the temple to worship. I do not inquire
Beyond the faith, beyond the willingness
To embrace the faith."—"And what," he said, "is the faith?"
She said to him softly: "Look about you." He looked
At effigies, paintings, showing modes of love
Not known to Israel, she talking the while,
Holding a torch to light the effigies:
"The faith is love, but not perhaps love
As a desert people will know it. You desert folk
Live in wide space and feel a desire to fill it.
You are a nation, so I hear, that is desirous
Of being great among the peoples of the earth.
You breed, you fill your tents with children. With you
The coupling of man and woman is to that end.
You do not talk or dream of the ecstasy of love—
Only the seed's flow, the setting of the seed to work.
To you, the act of the man and woman is like the
Sowing of a field. To us, it is not so."
Zimri gulped at some of the effigies.
"Whatever it is, this love of yours, it is an
Abomination before the Lord."—"Which Lord?" she asked.
Zimri said: "There is only one —our God,
The creator and sustainer of the world,
The God of Israel, the God of mankind."
She smiled. "The God of a madman on a donkey—
That is how he appears to the Moabites.
But you must see what we mean by love. Come with me."
He cried out: "No. Blasphemy. Filth." She said:
"It is blasphemy and filth to know that ecstasy
Which divides men from the beasts of the field? It is
Blasphemy and filth to know oneself

In the very living presence of the god?
The ecstasy is sent by the god: it is blasphemy
To reject it. The cleanness of the spirit,
From which all earthly dross is purged away—
To reject that is the sin of wallowing
In the filth of the animals." But Zimri cried: "No. No."
But he suffered himself, saying *no no* the while,
To be led to the inner temple, drawn there
In his own despite. The priestess ordered, with a gesture,
Two servants to open the portal. Then he saw.
He saw, before an effigy of Ba'al
As god of love, votive lamps burning. He heard
Flutes and a harp, incense boats clanging, smelt
The richness of roasting herbs. Above all, he saw.
His eyes throbbed at the sight of the men, exalted
In a kind of holiness of lust, prostrating themselves
Before the prospect of love, before the flesh
Of the temple houris. He saw them, evil beauty,
And saw eyes on himself. They stood there, naked,
Before unseeing Ba'al. Zimri moaned, fled, blinded.
And the priestess said, as he fumbled at the portal:
"Well, Israelite—are you prepared
To become not an Israelite but merely
A worshipper at the shrine? You are heartily welcome."
But he cried out: "No. No." Blindly stumbling
Down the steps of the temple, jostled and jostling
Along a street of the city (*no no*), followed by laughter,
Obscenity, out of the city by its gate,
Back to the camp, hearing ring in his head
Moabite voices crooning about love.
He lay alone in his tent, writhing (*no
No*), and pale in the morning, went to Joshua
To render a report. Joshua said:
"Filthy pagan rites. Any evidence
Of our people indulging in filthy pagan rites?"
Zimri said: "I thought I saw—but no matter.
Nothing as yet really to report.
Wait. I am watchful."—"We know you are watchful, Zimri.
We call you Zimri the incorruptible."

Was there a sneer in the voice? He went again,
That night, to the temple. The priestess greeted him:
"The Israelite. Is this more official business?"
Zimri said: "I come with a warning. If
Any of our people—engage—in your rites,
You yourselves will be in danger." She smiled:
"You mean the Israelite god of love and justice
Will wipe us all out with the sword?" Zimri said:
"Admit none of our people. You who talk of love
Should not desire to see love followed by pain.
But they will be punished, I warn you. I am watching."
She said: "Well, if your priests and priestesses
(Do you have priestesses? I am somewhat ignorant
About your faith)—if, I say, they are willing
To persuade us to the superior attractions
Of your god, then we will be ready to listen.
Conversions are made in men's hearts and men's loins.
They are not easily enforced with armies and thunder."
Zimri said: "I warn. It is a warning."
From out of the temple two men came with obeisances
To the priestess. They recognized Zimri, being Israelites,
But he had his eyes to the ground, unwilling
To meet hers, despite his "Warning, a solemn warning."
The Israelites rushed away, and Zimri, emerging,
Saw men running, but did not know who they were.
So, watchful Zimri, he wandered the town in torment,
Not knowing his feeling—anger, lust, envy—
Not knowing what he felt but knowing its violence,
And he came to a tavern and drank of the wine of Moab,
Hearing song, drank of the wine till a girl came
To ask if he would drink yet more of the wine,
Of the wine more, more of the, Moab the wine of,
More. But no. He shook his head and could not
Stop shaking it. No. *I warn. A warning. Solemn.*
"So," the priestess said, "you are very persistent.
Another solemn warning?" For he was back there,
His tongue thick, tottering, shaking his head,
Not able to stop shaking it, hearing laughter,
Then hearing the laughter cease, hearing himself

Fall to the floor, hearing, feeling nothing.
Servants came forward, solicitous, to raise him.
He was helped away to a bed somewhere, and the priestess,
Smiling with the sadness of long knowledge,
Said: "As so often happens, he finds his way
Through the little god of wine towards the great god:
Blessed then be the little god," seeing him there,
Smirking on the wall, crowned with vine leaves,
The great god waiting apart, master and servant,
Humbly on Zimri's awakening. *Most blessed be he.*

17 | ABOMINATIONS BEFORE THE LORD

ZIMRI emerged from the cave and saw bright morning
Beyond the casement—a fountain, oleanders—
And flooding the chamber, wondering where he was
And then remembering the waking in the night,
Her beside him. She now, with eyes laughing,
Poured from a pitcher into a cup. She said:
"You have slept long and deep. Take this," bringing it.
"Take. It is no poison." Herbs, achingly pungent,
Vied with dried rose petals on the bed where he lay.
He drank, tasting herbs and petals, seeing the cup
Cunningly embossed with arms and bosoms,
Then probed in his mind for shame but found none. She
Lay by him in a loose robe, her eyes laughing,
Her hair loose, a torrent of bronze. "Your name," he said.
"I forget your name, or did I hear your name?"
She told him he had heard it—Cozbi, daughter
Of a minor prince of Moab whose name did not matter,
Servant of Ba'al. "Daughter of a prince,"
He said, "and you are here."—"But this is holy work,"
She told him. "We are not street girls. What we do
Is in honor of the god. We call it holy work—
To bring men closer to the god." She kissed him then,
Holy work. "We are the chosen ones.
Not every woman can take her place in the temple.
Today you are specially blessed, I also,
For today is a feast day of the god. You came to us
On the eve of his feast day: it was as if you knew."

Ba'al, genially ferocious, in hammered bronze,
Was carried about the town that day, drums beating,
Trumpets and shawms braying, flutes cooing,
Some of his votaries drunk, all half-naked,
Honoring the god. Two Israelite officers,
Biting their lips, watching the procession,
Looking for— "An abomination," said one.
"Look at them—look at that couple there."—"I see them,"
The other said, seeing them. "But what can we do?
The Moabites are not our responsibility—"
"But those are," said the first, pointing. "Look at them."
Israelites, drunk and gay, dancing along.
"Some of ours," said the other. "I see what you mean.
But can we make an arrest? Now?" The first one gloomed,
Envy perhaps in his gloom. "I see what you mean.
They'd tear us to pieces, man." As night fell,
The Moabites set up their bronze Ba'al high on a plinth,
And the revelers danced about, in contrary circles,
A contradance, singing something filthy and ancient,
Ending exhausted on the sward, any with all,
Man with boy with woman with man with, not too exhausted
To frot away, very holy work, while the god grinned.
But in daylight, in the garden of the temple,
Jasmine, oleander, fountains, birdsong,
Zimri saw holiness of a different order,
Walking, fingers entwined, with Cozbi, saying:
"Why was I so slow in learning?"—"You were not slow—"
"I mean, I mean, why did it never occur to me,
Or to any of our people, that truly we worship
A god of misery, a god who hates all joy?
I see the truth clearly now. A god descended
When first we lay together, and it was not our God,
Not the God of the Israelites. Yet this god,
Or goddess as it may be, is a true god,
Laughing, benign . . ."—"The god will descend again,
Any time we call on him—or her,"
Cozbi said, "for Ba'al is both she and he,
Mother and father, taking a lover's lineaments,
All things to us." He embraced her lovingly,

Saying: "A new misery torments me.
You will leave me. You will give yourself to others."
She said: "That may seem strange to you. To us
It is a sacred duty."—"But, beloved, might it not be
A duty more sacred to be my love, my one love?
If there is a god of love, there must also be
A god of marriage."—"The gods," she said, "do not
Concern themselves with marriage. Marriage is for
The making of children, the fixing of—what is the word?"
He said: "Inheritances. Land. Wealth. Cattle.
Maintaining the power of a family. That is true.
But I have seen with my own eyes a god shine out
From the bodies of girls and boys who have entered marriage.
She said: "For how long? The god yawns after a time
And then departs. Or he reveals himself
As a god of bitterness. In our temple
There is only the ecstasy."—"But you," he said,
"You are not just the vessel of the ecstasy.
You are yourself—you are my one dear love.
Love is not something out there, not a passage of joy
Between people who have no names. Love is ourselves.
Love is a word invented for us and us only.
The God is alive only when you and I
Lie embraced, alone, the world shut out."
She said: "Our high priestess would call that heresy."
But he: "Yet she would smile when saying the word,
As you are smiling now." So they embraced,
And his eyes watered with love, his limbs trembled.
While *out there*, in the city, a great banquet
In honor of Ba'al proceeded—spitting roasts,
Wine spilling. "Eat," cried the host. "Eat ye.
For this is the very flesh of the god Ba'al,
Whose name be blessed in the ten worlds forever.
Eat, eat and do homage, for he is here
In the flesh of the lands and seas, in the birds that sing,
In the beasts that grunt, in the armored fish of the waters.
Eat, eat: do homage to his greatness."
And they ate and belched their praise. Moses heard of it,
Moses heard all from the moral patrols and cried:

"Every abomination that defiled them
With the worship of the golden calf—worse, you tell me,
Since they are eating of filthy forbidden flesh—
Scavengers of the sea, filled with dirt,
Pig flesh, milk and flesh meat in the one vessel.
Who has allowed this to happen? Speak. Who?
And he looked at Joshua, Caleb, Eleazar,
The patrol leaders, but none said anything,
And their silence was in manner of a rebuke.
Sighing, he said: "It is, at the last, myself—
The bad shepherd who has let the lambs go astray.
I have had a bereavement to suffer, a black season
Of mourning and solitude. But Joshua, my son,
You who must take up the rod of office, you
Who must bear the burden of leadership, Joshua,
How is it possible?" Joshua spoke softly.
"There were reports of particular transgressions.
Action was taken. As for the recent events—
Information was slow in coming. We had no
Word from Zimri. We understood all was well,
More or less well. Odd acts of delinquency.
But nothing that seemed to require major action."
Moses said: "Where is Zimri?"—"No one knows.
We surmise that he may have been killed, because of his zeal.
They are an unruly people, the people of Moab."
Moses said: "He was of good family.
I knew his father well. Honest, steadfast,
Pious. Now, Joshua, what do you propose?"
Joshua said: "Some of our erring people
Have already come home, ashamed and sick.
Ready for punishment. I suppose we must march in,
Ferret out the others. Or perhaps show
Our power and our righteousness. Punish the whole town.
Massacre. Set fire to it. Though, to speak truly,
We have had enough of such wholesale slaughter."
Moses said: "The time for a judgment on Moab
Must come later, come in the Lord's own time.
Meanwhile, our punishments for our erring sons
Must be," he said, "exemplary."—"Exemplary—how?"

Moses said: "The word will come to me.
I fear it will be a harsh word." Harsh word, harsh,
And more than a harsh word. Cozbi was weeping
In Zimri's arms, in the room of a squalid inn.
He said, not unhappily: Punishment
For loving too well. Or it may be a reward."
She said: "I was always told," then she wept again,
"It was not for the weak of heart." But he said: "Strong,
Strong of heart. Is not this love of ours
Better, holier, than all that nonsense of the temple,
That wickedness of the temple?" She spoke of dishonor.
"You do not understand the dishonor." Harsh words
From the high priestess. "How can I show my face
Again in the streets, in my father's house? The god
Has turned his back on me." Zimri kissed her tears.
"You have found out in time, through the grace of some
                  other god,
That you were not meant for that service. And yet,
                  of course,
It was that which brought us together. The world
          is strange,
God is strange." She said: "Which god do you mean?"
He said: "Who knows? Perhaps the God of my people.
What kind of," he said, "malediction
Did your high priestess pronounce on you?"
Cozbi sobbed again. "She said that I had
Disgraced the temple, but then she admitted
Her own share of the blame. After all, it was she who
Encouraged me to to . . ." Zimri smiled:
"Seduce me to a religion of love? There, you are smiling.
And you, my love, a princess among your people,
Shall be an even higher princess among mine.
So all shall end well." They kissed and then she said:
"Where is this promised land you talk about?"
He said: "Beyond the Jordan. Even now
The work of parceling out the land goes on.
To my tribe comes a great tract of rich soil,
Rich grass. We shall build a fair palace of stone
And live in love forever and ever." Then she said:

"You must know now—but surely you already know—
That I may not have children. The temple of love
Was given over to joy, not fertility."
But he cried: "What does it matter? Israel
Can grow and flourish with no need of our help.
We shall be a new twin star in its sky.
That word *barren*—it is meant as a word of shame,
But the moon is barren and its light shines on the earth
With a beauty that the sun does not know. As now."
He embraced her tenderly. "We are moon lovers."
She said: "We must leave early. Put out the light."
So he doused the lamp, saying however: "The light
Can never be put out." And the moon
Embraced them who embraced each other. *Never
Be put out.* In harsh sunlight Moses
Addressed the multitude: "You, children of Israel,
Have committed whoredoms with the daughters of Moab.
You have sacriced to their gods, you have eaten
Of foul flesh and bowed down to Ba'al.
The anger of the Lord is a burning torrent.
For he is the one God, the God of mankind,
Who made mankind and all the earth and the heavens,
And he is a jealous God.
And his word has come to me, and this is his word."
The sinners waited, rightly apprehensive,
The troops stern behind them. Moses said:
"His word is this: *Take all the heads of the people
That have sinned, and hang them before the Lord,
Up against the sun, that the Lord's fierce anger
May be turned away from Israel.* Judges," he cried.
And the judges, shocked but ready, looked towards him.
"Judges, you have heard the order of the Lord.
Let justice be done." So Moses turned away
While justice was done, shutting his ears to torment
And curses, the terrified voices that cried:
*The God of Jacob is a God of butchers
And Moses is the chief of butchers,* saying:
"I spoke too soon when I said the work was over.
I see now that the work is never over.

But, Lord God, may my work soon be over."
The lovers stood, puzzled, when they came to the encampment,
Finding weeping and rending of garments by the tabernacle,
Then they looked up and saw. "Is this what they do?"
Cried Cozbi in fear. "Is this the kind of
Thing that the Israelites do?" Zimri said: "Justice,"
In a weak voice. "They have been seeking justice.
But for what crime?" Cozbi cried: "Let us go.
Back to the city." But Joshua was upon them,
An armed squad behind him, saying: "So.
You came back to us, Zimri. With, as I see,
One of the whores of Moab." Zimri cried out:
"Guard your tongue. The *whore* to whom you refer
Is the daughter of a prince of Moab, head
Of a great house in the kingdom. She is also my bride—"
"Your *bride*," Joshua said. "That is a stage
Further than whoredom. You are both under arrest."
Zimri said stoutly: "On what charge?" And Joshua:
"Abominations before the Lord our God—"
"Wait," Zimri said, "was I not sent to the city
On your own instructions? What proof do you possess
That I have committed *whoredoms*, as you call them?"
"The proof," said Joshua, "stands beside you." Zimri,
In a voice that rang out, said: "Ah, Joshua,
You who love the law so much that
Severed heads must grin in the sun for it,
You shall have the law, but she and I
Will have it too. For which of our laws forbids
The converting of a pagan to the faith?
What law forbids the marriage of an Israelite
To the daughter of a foreign people?" Joshua,
More doubtfully than before: "The situation
Is, at best, highly suspicious."—"I see.
Suspicion is enough for arrest, for threat,
For insult?"—"The judges," now said Joshua, "must decide.
In the meantime, you are both under arrest.
On suspicion which, to a people at war, is enough.
And, if you will accept the word of our leader,
Which is also enough, the people of Moab,

From newborn child to doddering graybeard, are
Defined by him as an unclean people, source
Of disease of body and of spirit." Zimri said:
"Do not talk to me of uncleanness, Joshua.
You smell of blood, blood, which, I fear,
Will not easily be washed out."—"No more talk.
Place them in the guard tents. Separately."
But Zimri countered: "Wait. I claim, by right,
The protection of my own tribe." Joshua: "No.
The law of the whole people cancels out
The laws and customs of the tribes."—"Is that then
Written on the tablets? I think not.
The ancient custom of wedlock with the Simeonites
Demands that the bride be brought before the people
To be approved of the people." Joshua said:
"Go, then. I am heartily sick of this matter.
It shall be left to the judges. But, Zimri, there will be
No escape. The perimeter guards have their orders."
Now it happened that a new priest, freshly appointed,
Spoke that night to the people: "My name is Phinehas.
I know I am the youngest of your priests,
But the fire of faith burns the stronger therefor,
Nor is authority nor wisdom thereby abated.
I speak to you of the primal vessel of sin,
Woman. Sin and impurity. Of woman."
But some of the women hearing hardened their faces
At his words, and at the words that followed:
"It was Eve, the mother of all mankind,
That brought sin into the world, and that sin rests
With all her daughters, sin made manifest
In their uncleanness—filth of the mensal courses,
Of the very process of birth. Far more than men,
Women are lodged in the flesh and cling to the flesh,
Are rarely roused to climb to the pure spirit.
If all women be unclean, how much more so
Are the women of the pagan peoples, in whom
Dwells the active devil of disruption—
The desire to draw men down from their purity
Into the stinking pit." Moses said

To Caleb: "I think he goes too far." But he listened:
"Within our very gates still lies the stench
Of foreign idols and all their abominations,
Reeking from a vessel of pagan filth.
I demand that the vessel be shattered." A woman cried:
"You spit on your own mother." And Moses said:
"He does go too far." But Phinehas, inflamed,
Cried out: "The curse of the all-highest fall
On all who shut their ears to the voice of holiness.
May they who harken not to the words of their priests
Be thrust to the bottomless pit of the fires that fail not,
To the eternal dungeons of divine damnation."
There was much more of this, but Cozbi,
Impure pagan vessel, and Zimri lay
In the peace of after-love, but a troubled peace.
"Believe me," he said, "beloved, all will change
When we have crossed the river. There will be no more
Suspicion, hatred, panic. Our people tremble
With fear and disordered nerves." But she: "Your people—
The members of your tribe—they like me?" Zimri:
"Did they not show as much? We talk of nation,
But the reality does not lie out there—
With armies, flags and tablets of the law.
It is in the tribe, which is but a family.
You are become a part of it." A shadow
Crossed them at that instant, obscuring the moon
An instant. Zimri said: "Who is there?" And Cozbi
Whispered: "Are they setting spies on us?"
A voice was over them, in their tent, shouting:
"A spy of the Lord God. Prepare, you, woman,
To join your stinking idols in the abode of blackness—"
"Who are you?" Zimri cried, rising aghast,
Arms out. Then there was a knife to be seen. "And you, too,
Son of the prince Salu and foul shame
To the tribe of Simeon." He lunged, Zimri fought,
The strength of the fanatic prevailed. Struck down,
Blood welling, he lay. Cozbi, in fear and horror,
Cried to the moon. "And now," Phinehas panted,
"Whore of Moab—" A scream through the sleeping camp,

Unheeded, some beast or bird of the night. At daybreak,
Phinehas spoke with pride of his work. *Zeal, zeal—*
The zeal of them who love the Lord. "Your zeal,"
Cried Moses. "Yes, your sacred zeal, as you call it.
But sacred zeal can go too far. I am sickened
By your sacred murderous zeal." But the priest, surprised,
Said: "We are an embattled people. Are not those your words?
The speck in the fruit corrupts the whole basket.
The accursed of God may be stricken down by the priests
        of God.
That is laid down in the law." But Moses said:
"The law is written on stone—hard, unyielding—
But the law may still be as flexible as a song.
Examine your own heart, Phinehas. You took pleasure
In the slaying of that innocent woman."—"Innocent?
Innocent?"—"Yes, she knew no better.
She was not one of the chosen. But perhaps
She was being drawn towards the light and the truth. Yet you
Took pleasure in slaying her perhaps because she was a woman.
You fear women, hence you see them as vessels of sin.
But I say this to you, Phinehas: that it is the women
Who will carry our faith when the men waver. Strength
Is in the woman and not in the man. Men dream,
But the divine vision is no dream. It is as real
As the sweeping of the hearth, real as the bearing of children.
The bones of women are strong to bear. Has the Lord
Spoken to you since your act of religious zeal?"
Phinehas said: "The Lord has sent dreams of sin
And dreams of killing. Then I wake howling." Moses
Shook his head: "You were not meant to be a priest.
A warrior perhaps. Well, you may soon be able
To plunge your steel into flesh less yielding. The news
Of your *zeal* may already have reached the divan of Balak."
But Phinehas: "She was a whore and a foul whore—"
Moses spat. "Go from me, little man.
What do you know about whores?"
                                    The apportioning
Of the land that they were yet to see went on.
Caleb read out the figures of the census, for the grant

Was to be by numbers: "The sons of Benjamin—
Forty-five thousand and six hundred. The families
Of the Shuhamites—sixty-four thousand four hundred.
Asher—the return is not yet in." Moses said:
"Not one who was with us in the desert of Sinai.
Not one who remembers Egypt. Except Joshua
And you. And me, but my day is over. The word
Of the Lord is fulfilled." Caleb, impatiently:
"Yes, yes. The families of Naphtali—little difference
In their numbers from the numbers of Benjamin—two hundred.
One might as well give them the same apportionment."
Clerks were at work on a planed board. Eleazar,
The son of Aaron, supervised, marking proportion,
Location. Then women approached, and Caleb said:
"Women? What can women want?" Five women,
Making with purpose towards Moses. Eleazar frowned:
"This is irregular. Women should stay with their children
And with their pots and pans." Moses said:
"You have been infected by the misplaced zeal
Of your former colleague. Where is he now, by the way?"
"Phinehas?" Eleazar frowned still. "Out with the army.
He has a gift for fighting."—"He will enjoy it,"
Moses sighed, "slaying the Midianite women.
God help us, when shall we ever be at peace?"
Eleazar said: "The holy war goes on.
Slay them, said the Lord. Feed the earth
With the blood of the idolator."—"Enough, Eleazar,"
Moses said, and then: "Welcome, daughters—"
"This is highly irregular," cried the priest.
"Many things are irregular," said one of the women.
"Including what we are about to speak about.
If it is permitted." Moses said:
"It is certainly permitted. You are, are you not,
The daughters of, the daughters of— Forgive me,
An old man's memory, or lack of it."
The woman said: "I am Mahlah. These are my sisters:
Hoglah, Noah, Milcah, Tirzah—daughters of
Zelophehad, now dead."—"Ah, yes," said Moses.
"Slain in battle, was he not?"—"Slain.

With his sons, our brothers. Thanks to your holy wars,
We are without menfolk. Though how a war can be holy—"
Eleazar said: "Have a care, woman," but she:
"Killing, killing, killing. Will your God
Strike me down because I cry against killing?
Well, let him. He is made in the likeness of a man."
Gently Moses said: "God is a spirit.
His voice has come to me in many forms,
Because a spirit lacks a voice of its own.
The voice has sometimes been the voice of Miriam,
My own sister." Mahlah said: "Be that as it may,
Your God seems fond of killing. A woman brings forth
With pain, high priest, that few men could truly bear—
Only that her sons may be killed in some holy war.
But that is not directly to my purpose—"
"What," said Moses gently, "is your purpose?"
Mahlah said: "We are women without menfolk.
The name of our father has disappeared from your record.
What will happen to his portion of the promised land?"
Eleazar said: "Woman, it is clearly laid down
That the sons alone shall inherit. If there are no sons,
There is no inheritance." But Mahlah cried:
"Injustice, man's injustice." And Eleazar:
"It is the law."—"That is always the answer:
It is the law. And how if the law be unjust?"
Eleazar said: "You merit the Lord's malediction.
One does not question the law." But she, in anger:
"High priest, I am questioning it." And Moses:
"Daughter, you are right to question it.
Peace, Eleazar. And my response is this:
If a man die and leave no son, then the father's
Inheritance shall pass to the daughters." Eleazar
Seemed ready to burn. "Heresy?" Moses said.
"An abomination? The Lord, as you see, high priest,
Has not yet offered to strike me dead. Nor will he.
Daughters of Israel, you have your inheritance."
But still in the future, always, it seemed, in the future.
Across the plain, soon, advancing armies,
And Joshua said: "They are coming for revenge.

Or shall we call it a pretext? You, priest,
Are certainly in the fight," addressing Phinehas
Who, stripped of his sacerdotal robes,
Arrayed as a somewhat puny warrior,
Sweated as he heard drums. Moses said:
"Is this the last battle, Joshua?
For all the kings of Midian will join Balak.
Evi and Rekem and Zur and Hur and Reba—"
"The last fight," Joshua said, "this side of Jordan.
How do the words go? Speak the words again—"
"The false gods crushed under the feet of Israel.
And you shall take the spoils of all their cattle
And all their flocks, yea, and all their goods,
And burn all the cities wherein they dwell.
A holy war, but we have not provoked it."
Joshua said: "You are tired. Stay in your tent.
I will send word." And Moses: "You will prevail.
The blessing of God go with you, Joshua."
So banners, trumpets and drums proclaimed to the sky
The going forth of the Israelites to war,
While Moses prayed: "Let there be an end to war—
An end, O Lord," but little hope in his words.

18 | JORDAN

Moses half-slept in his lonely tent—Gershom,
His son, gone with the army; Zipporah, his wife,
Dust; himself soon to be dust. He heard
His own voice, or the voice of the Lord, or of Israel:
And you have taken the spoils of all their cattle
And all their sheep, yea, and all their goods,
And burnt all the cities wherein they dwelt,
And all their goodly castles with fire and
All their goodly castles with fire and all their
Goodly castles with fire and he saw a
Castle innumerable cubits high falling
In flames and heard the screams of men falling,
Women and children. He came sharply awake
To sense a presence not a dreaming presence
And said: "Is it you, Lord?" And the presence said:
"All is fulfilled. The slain lie like leaves
In the fall tempests. Over those fallen leaves
You may fare forward. But first the sheep need
A new shepherd. Take Joshua, son of Nun,
A man in whom the spirit burns like a fire,
And lay your hand on him." So Joshua, from the wars,
Scarred and ready for wine and a handmaiden,
Was told these words and at once was hushed and solemn.
Before the tabernacle Moses laid his hand
On the warrior's head, saying: "You are not exalted
To any priesthood. You need no robes, no chrism.
You are become that humblest of beings—a leader

Accountable to the people and to the Lord,
With duties and no rights." He raised his arms
Before the assembled nation, bidding them
Acclaim their new shepherd, hearing however
Beneath the acclamation the growls of the restive,
As was to be expected. He smiled with relief
At being allowed the guerdon of fatigue,
Old age at last. Under a star-filled heaven
Their caravan moved in silence, under the sun,
Moses at rest in an oxcart, Joshua ahead,
Until one day Joshua came and pointed
Ahead at a certain mountain. Pisgah? Pisgah.
So in the plain they set up the tabernacle,
Pitched their tents, the people in good heart,
The young singing and dancing about the fires,
Moses fulfilling his last duties. He said,
To the tribal leaders round a fire, plain words
About the necessity and beauty of the law
Or laws: "Too many laws, some will say—
A huge web woven of many webs—but remember
This, this: that the law is our city,
Complex, cunningly woven—many streets,
Buildings, rooms—yet a city we may carry
About with us, wherever we go. Remember
This: we are the chosen, and this means
Many enemies among the unchosen. Enemies.
They will slay us and pursue us. The unchosen.
And we may never finally be at rest.
But wherever we go we will carry our city with us.
The law. Break one single stone of the law,
However small, and a part of the city falls.
Soon the temples and palaces and dwellings
Will crash about our ears. And we shall be lost.
Keep the law. Teach the law. *Teach it.*"
Phinehas, a subdued man, lacking an arm,
Stiff with scars, taught the children, asking:
"What are we allowed to eat?" *The ox*
The sheep the goat the roebuck "If you were asked
What kind of animal?" *Animals that have their*
Hoof parted in two "Like the pig?"

No no no no "Why not like the pig?"
Because the pig does not chew the cud
"So the animal has to chew the cud. So we may
Eat the camel, the rabbit, the hare?" *No no*
No no no "Why not?" *Because they do not*
Divide the hoof in two "So we can
Eat beasts that divide the hoof and chew the cud,
But not beasts that just do one and not both.
Yes, my son?" *Why?* "Well, let me put it
This way . . ." Eleazar taught older boys,
Saying: "Well, let me put it this way.
Without the past the present can mean nothing.
Without the past a man is a sort of ghost
Trembling on the brink of a future
He cannot understand. So we remember
The past in ceremonies, force ourselves to remember.
In our promised land we shall remember
Our long exile, tribulations, thus
Becoming aware of our qualities as a nation,
A fighting nation, a law-abiding nation,
A proud nation." *Rabbi—* "Yes, my son?"
Why isn't Moses going with us? "Well now,
Let me put it this way . . ." Moses was saying,
Addressing the priests and elders: "Because of my doubt
Of God's promise, because I cried out on my trust
And sought to reject it, I may not enter. You
Shall cross the Jordan, Joshua leading you,
But I—full of years, at the end of my journey—
Must await my end here. But I have taught you
The song I have written. Teach it. Remember it.
Remember me." So they taught it, and one day
The whole of the people sang it, the song of Moses:
"Give ear, O ye heavens, and I will speak.
And hear, O earth, the words of my mouth.
My doctrine shall drop as the rain,
My speech shall distill as the dew,
As the small rain upon the tender herb,
And as the showers upon the grass.
The Lord is the Rock, his work is perfect.
Rejoice, O ye nations, with his people:

For he will avenge the blood of his servants,
And will be merciful unto his land,
And to his people." They danced to the flute, the harp,
The shawm, the trumpet, to the air of his song:

And Moses said: "Beloved, keep the commandments.
Love justice and mercy. Love the Lord our God,
For his ways are the ways of justice and mercy."
And he saw that the time was coming for his people
To pass over the river and take up their inheritance.
So he bade the whole of the Israelite nation kneel,
And they knelt, and then he blessed them, saying:
"Happy art thou, O Israel. Who is like unto thee,
O people saved by the Lord, the shield of thy help
And the sword of thy excellency. There is none like unto
        your God,
Who rides upon the heavens. The eternal God
Is your refuge, and underneath
Are the everlasting arms." Then the Israelite army
Saluted his greatness with shouts and with the clamor
Of drums and silver trumpets. So he moved
To the mountain, and Caleb and Joshua tried to help him
In his climb to its summit, but he waved their help aside.
He climbed and they watched him, thinking: *Strong as an ox,
With the eyes of an eagle,* but it was not true,
Not true any longer. The Israelites, shielding their sight
Against the sun, watched him long and long
Till he reached the top of the mountain. There he rested.
And after a time of rest he heard a voice,
His own voice, young again, saying unto him:
"Now, Moses, I will show you their inheritance."
He said: "But not mine," with his old boldness,
The boldness of a prince. "You are a hard
And unforgiving God." The voice said. "Unforgiving?

If you but knew, if you only knew. But I
Have sworn and made my covenant with man.
I shall not again destroy him for his sins.
Yet I shall torment him with dissatisfaction,
For only in me shall he be satisfied.
Look now—all the land of Gilead, unto Dan."
And Moses stood to look, seeing the river,
And all the lands beyond the river, fair,
Rich and fair. "Look. And all Naphtali
And the land of Ephraim and Manasseh,
And the land of Judah, unto the utmost sea.
And the plain of the valley of Jericho, city of palm trees,
Unto Zoar. This is the land which I swore
Unto Abraham, and Isaac, and unto Jacob,
Saying: I will give it unto thy seed.
Moses, I have caused thee to see it with thine eyes,
But thou shalt not go thither." Moses did not
Weep, but he said again, with a princely boldness:
"You are a hard and unforgiving God—"
"Go down now. Return to the valley of Moab,"
Said the voice. And Moses said: "To die."
And the voice said: "What else?" So he went down
And waited, willing death, which was not long,
For when a man's work is done there is only death.
The women closed his eyes, wailing, but Joshua
Was dry-eyed. Eleazar made an obeisance
To the leader of the Israelites, and said:
"You must give the instructions as to his burial."
And Joshua said: "Here in this valley of Moab,
This side of Jordan." And then Eleazar said:
"You must now give instructions as to the gravestone
And what shall be written thereon." But Joshua said:
"It is better that no man know where he is buried.
It is better that he be thought of as—
Not lying in one place. For he must not be
Worshipped as an idol. We must not have
Idolators at his shrine. He is with us
In the water we drink, the food we eat. We breathe him."
Eleazar said: "Will you make up the words
That shall be spoken to the people?" But Joshua:

"I have already made them." And so he spoke to the people:
"There will never arise again in Israel
A prophet like unto Moses, whom the Lord
Knew face to face. In all the signs and wonders,
Which the Lord sent him to do in the land of Egypt
To Pharaoh and to all his servants and to all his land,
And in all that mighty hand, and the great terror
Which Moses showed in the sight of all Israel."
The muffled drums beat, and the body of Moses
Was borne away on a litter. Many of the people
Wished to follow, but Joshua forbade them.
The body of Moses was carried none knows whither
And rests now none knows where. *And Joshua
The son of Nun was full of the spirit of wisdom.
For Moses had laid his hands upon him,
And the children of Israel harkened unto him,
And did as the Lord commanded Moses.* Joshua
Raised his blessed hand, and they fared forward,
Coming at length to a river. Caleb said:
"At last." But Joshua: "We still have to cross it.
God will provide. This is only a river.
Once we crossed a sea. Well—we have our orders."
He smiled, and Caleb smiled, and so they marched.
And then, at last, the voice spoke to Joshua:
"Moses my servant is dead. Now therefore, Joshua,
Go over this Jordan, thou, and all this people
Unto the land which I do give them. From the wilderness
Even unto the great river, the Euphrates,
And unto the great sea towards the going down
Of the sun. And as I was with Moses,
So will I be with thee: I will not fail thee,
Nor forsake thee. Be therefore not afraid,
Neither be thou dismayed, for the Lord thy God
Is with thee whithersoever thou goest." The wilderness
Held a grave, but none would know the grave.
Not from the grave but from the living air
And the beating blood of Israel the voice
Of the living Moses echoed: *For the Lord
Thy God is with thee whithersoever thou goest.*

ANTHONY BURGESS, at present furiously or plaintively ageing on the lake of Bracciano near Rome, and proposing to become an old man with a panama and little dog in Monaco, was born in Manchester, England. Like many Mancunians, especially when they have Irish blood and a Catholic background, he finds the Mediterranean more congenial than the Thames, and he left the London literary and journalistic life behind eight years ago to get on with some real work. Ironically, he has been spending much of his time on film-scripts and other commissioned chores and has added little to the fairly large oeuvre he had already achieved or excreted before leaving England. He is trying to write a very long novel about the late Pope John, as seen from the angle of a homosexual writer like Somerset Maugham, but other things get in the way—as for instance the next Universal disaster film, ultimate really as it is about the end of the world. He has also been brought back into the field of music, where he started his artistic career, and his third symphony was performed in Iowa City in October, 1975. He is contemplating, among other things, the composition of an opera on George III.

The fictional works he has written since leaving England comprise a big historical novel called *Napoleon Symphony*, the third item in his Enderby trilogy, *The Clockwork Testament*, and a novel that no British critic except Frank Kermode understood—*M/F*, the first fictional piece to be based on the structuralist theories of Claude Lévi-Strauss. The little book entitled *A Long Trip to Teatime*, which is ostensibly for children, is structuralist in that its narrative has been made up out of a section of an encyclopedia—

viz., it relies on what a letter of the alphabet can provide and not on a plot devised by the imagination.

Mr. Burgess, having just done a counting job around his bookshelves, discovers that he has published something like thirty books, apart from editions of and introductions to the work of other writers. His fecundity has been regarded by more gentlemanly authors as an affront to the tradition of elegantly spare output best exemplified in E. M. Forster. His response to this is that one must write much if one is to earn a living by writing, and that, if one works hard enough, there is no reason why grace and shapeliness should be incompatible with prolificity. He is aware that he is not greatly liked in England. Geoffrey Grigson, the *Country Life* reviewer and poet, found the personality revealed in his work "coarse and unattractive." This is an extreme expression of a pretty widely held attitude which makes Mr. Burgess's thumb shake with rage as it counts the banknotes which he periodically takes from under the mattress of one or other of his many houses.

The older he grows, the more Mr. Burgess is convinced that our salvation lies in understanding ourselves, that such understanding depends on a concern with language, and that such concern is dying in contemporary England. One expects a tasteful poetaster to be made Poet Laureate: since Dryden this has been traditional. But one does not expect to find an arbiter of literature praised for having a tin ear. Mr. Burgess mentions no names since he has already suffered two libel actions and been threatened with a third. It is a British writer's duty, he thinks, to get out of Britain if he can and examine the English language against the foil of other tongues, occasionally going back as a tourist and staying at Claridge's.

Mr. Burgess smokes excessively, having been encouraged to do so by a heavy-smoking professor emeritus of ninety-four he met in America who also drinks a pint of mixed Christian Brothers brandy and Roma Rocket daily. He cooks for his family, plays the piano, travels widely, but mostly writes. *A Long Trip to Teatime* is one of the things he has written recently, and translations of the obscene and blasphemous sonnets of the Roman poet Belli.

A.B.